55 Pork Recipes for Home

By: Kelly Johnson

Table of Contents

- Classic Pork Roast with Herbs
- Maple Glazed Pork Chops
- Garlic and Rosemary Grilled Pork Tenderloin
- Slow Cooker Pulled Pork
- Honey Mustard Glazed Ham
- Balsamic-Glazed Pork Loin
- Korean BBQ Pork Belly
- Apple Cider Braised Pork Shoulder
- Teriyaki Pork Stir-Fry
- Cajun Spiced Pork Ribs
- Cuban Mojo Pork
- Mediterranean Stuffed Pork Loin
- Pineapple and Soy-Glazed Pork Chops
- Thai Basil Pork Stir-Fry
- Beer-Braised Bratwurst
- Peach and Bourbon Glazed Pork Tenderloin
- Italian Sausage and Peppers
- Jamaican Jerk Pork
- Mustard and Brown Sugar Glazed Ham
- Szechuan-style Shredded Pork
- Apricot Glazed Pork Loin
- Chipotle Lime Pork Tacos
- Cider-Braised Pork Belly
- Filipino Adobo Pork
- Cranberry and Dijon Pork Roast
- Hoisin and Ginger Pork Skewers
- Southern BBQ Pulled Pork Sandwiches
- Lemon Garlic Butter Pork Chops
- Cuban Sandwich with Mojo-Marinated Pork
- Pineapple Teriyaki Pork Burgers
- Five-Spice Roast Pork Belly
- Pomegranate Glazed Pork Tenderloin
- German Sauerkraut and Pork
- Miso-Glazed Pork Belly
- Bacon-Wrapped Pork Medallions

- Moroccan Spiced Pork Tagine
- Caramelized Onion and Apple Stuffed Pork Chops
- Tex-Mex Pork Carnitas
- Fig and Port Wine Glazed Ham
- Thai Coconut Curry Pork
- Bourbon and Brown Sugar Pork Ribs
- Pesto-Stuffed Grilled Pork Chops
- Vietnamese Lemongrass Pork Banh Mi
- Raspberry Balsamic Glazed Pork Tenderloin
- Garlic Parmesan Crusted Pork Chops
- Pineapple Jalapeño Pulled Pork Sliders
- Greek Gyro with Pork Souvlaki
- Teriyaki Pineapple Pork Kebabs
- Cuban Picadillo with Ground Pork
- Mustard and Herb Crusted Pork Loin
- Spicy Mango Glazed Pork Chops
- Chipotle BBQ Pulled Pork Nachos
- Herb-Marinated Pork Skewers
- Cajun Dirty Rice with Ground Pork
- Apple Sage Stuffed Pork Chops

Classic Pork Roast with Herbs

Ingredients:

- 1 bone-in pork loin roast (about 4-5 pounds)
- 3 tablespoons olive oil
- 4 cloves garlic, minced
- 2 teaspoons dried rosemary
- 2 teaspoons dried thyme
- 1 teaspoon dried sage
- Salt and black pepper, to taste
- 1 cup chicken or vegetable broth
- 1/2 cup dry white wine (optional)

Instructions:

Preheat your oven to 350°F (175°C).
In a small bowl, mix together the minced garlic, rosemary, thyme, sage, salt, and black pepper to create the herb rub.
Pat the pork roast dry with paper towels. Rub the herb mixture all over the pork, ensuring an even coating.
Heat olive oil in a large oven-safe skillet or roasting pan over medium-high heat. Sear the pork roast on all sides until golden brown, about 3-4 minutes per side.
If using a skillet, transfer the pork roast to a preheated oven-safe roasting pan. Alternatively, you can use the skillet if it's oven-safe.
Pour the broth and wine (if using) into the pan, creating a flavorful base for basting.
Roast in the preheated oven for about 1.5 to 2 hours or until the internal temperature reaches 145°F (63°C). Baste the pork with the pan juices every 30 minutes.
Once cooked, remove the pork from the oven, cover loosely with aluminum foil, and let it rest for 15 minutes before slicing.
Slice the pork roast into desired thickness and serve with the pan juices as a delicious au jus.

This classic pork roast with herbs is a timeless dish that combines the simplicity of preparation with the rich flavors of rosemary, thyme, and sage. Perfect for a family dinner or special occasion, this roast will surely become a go-to recipe in your culinary repertoire. Enjoy!

Maple Glazed Pork Chops

Ingredients:

- 4 bone-in pork chops (about 1 inch thick)
- Salt and black pepper, to taste
- 2 tablespoons olive oil

For the Maple Glaze:

- 1/4 cup pure maple syrup
- 2 tablespoons Dijon mustard
- 2 tablespoons soy sauce
- 2 cloves garlic, minced
- 1 teaspoon fresh thyme leaves (or 1/2 teaspoon dried thyme)

Instructions:

Preheat your oven to 375°F (190°C).
Season the pork chops with salt and black pepper on both sides.
In a large oven-safe skillet, heat olive oil over medium-high heat.
Sear the pork chops for 3-4 minutes per side, or until they develop a golden brown crust. Transfer the skillet to the preheated oven.
While the pork chops are in the oven, prepare the maple glaze. In a small bowl, whisk together maple syrup, Dijon mustard, soy sauce, minced garlic, and thyme.
After the pork chops have cooked in the oven for about 10-12 minutes, brush them generously with the maple glaze.
Continue baking for an additional 5-7 minutes or until the internal temperature of the pork chops reaches 145°F (63°C) and the glaze is caramelized.
Remove the skillet from the oven and let the pork chops rest for a few minutes.
Spoon any remaining glaze from the skillet over the pork chops before serving.
Serve the maple glazed pork chops with your favorite sides, such as roasted vegetables, mashed potatoes, or a fresh salad.

These Maple Glazed Pork Chops strike the perfect balance between sweet and savory. The maple glaze adds a delightful caramelized coating to the pork, making this dish a deliciously memorable addition to your dinner table. Enjoy the rich flavors and succulence of these glazed pork chops!

Garlic and Rosemary Grilled Pork Tenderloin

Ingredients:

- 2 pork tenderloins (about 1 pound each)

- 4 cloves garlic, minced
- 2 tablespoons fresh rosemary, finely chopped (or 1 tablespoon dried rosemary)
- 3 tablespoons olive oil
- 2 tablespoons Dijon mustard
- 1 tablespoon soy sauce
- 1 teaspoon honey
- Salt and black pepper, to taste

Instructions:

Preheat your grill to medium-high heat.
Trim excess fat and silver skin from the pork tenderloins.
In a small bowl, combine minced garlic, chopped rosemary, olive oil, Dijon mustard, soy sauce, honey, salt, and black pepper to create the marinade.
Place the pork tenderloins in a large zip-top bag or a shallow dish and pour half of the marinade over them. Reserve the remaining marinade for basting.
Seal the bag or cover the dish and refrigerate for at least 30 minutes, allowing the flavors to infuse into the pork.
Remove the pork from the refrigerator and let it come to room temperature for about 15 minutes.
Preheat the grill to medium-high heat.
Remove the pork from the marinade, letting excess marinade drip off.
Grill the pork tenderloins for 15-20 minutes, turning occasionally, or until the internal temperature reaches 145°F (63°C).
During the last few minutes of grilling, brush the pork with the reserved marinade, creating a flavorful glaze.
Once cooked, transfer the pork tenderloins to a cutting board and let them rest for 5 minutes before slicing.
Slice the grilled pork tenderloin into medallions and serve with your favorite sides.

This Garlic and Rosemary Grilled Pork Tenderloin is a succulent and flavorful dish that combines the aromatic herbs with the smoky goodness of the grill. Perfect for a summer barbecue or a weeknight dinner, this recipe delivers a mouthwatering experience that will have your guests asking for seconds. Enjoy the tender and juicy results!

Slow Cooker Pulled Pork

Ingredients:

- 3-4 pounds pork shoulder or pork butt, trimmed of excess fat

- 1 large onion, thinly sliced
- 4 cloves garlic, minced
- 1 cup chicken broth
- 1/2 cup apple cider vinegar
- 1/3 cup soy sauce
- 1/4 cup brown sugar, packed
- 1 tablespoon smoked paprika
- 1 tablespoon chili powder
- 1 teaspoon cayenne pepper (adjust for spice preference)
- 1 teaspoon ground cumin
- Salt and black pepper, to taste

For Serving:

- Burger buns or your favorite sandwich rolls
- Coleslaw (optional)

Instructions:

Season the pork shoulder with salt and black pepper.
Place the sliced onions and minced garlic at the bottom of the slow cooker.
In a bowl, whisk together chicken broth, apple cider vinegar, soy sauce, brown sugar, smoked paprika, chili powder, cayenne pepper, and ground cumin.
Place the seasoned pork shoulder in the slow cooker and pour the liquid mixture over it.
Cover and cook on low for 8-10 hours or until the pork is tender and easily shreds with a fork.
Once cooked, remove the pork from the slow cooker and shred it using two forks. Remove excess fat if necessary.
Optionally, you can return the shredded pork to the slow cooker to absorb more of the flavorful juices.
Taste and adjust seasoning if needed. You can add more salt, pepper, or a touch of brown sugar for sweetness.
Serve the pulled pork on burger buns or sandwich rolls. Top with coleslaw if desired.
Enjoy your delicious and tender slow cooker pulled pork sandwiches!

This Slow Cooker Pulled Pork recipe offers a hassle-free way to achieve flavorful and tender pulled pork. The combination of spices and slow cooking creates a mouthwatering dish that's perfect for sandwiches, tacos, or served alongside your favorite side dishes. It's a crowd-pleaser for gatherings or an easy weeknight meal. Enjoy the convenience and deliciousness of slow-cooked pulled pork!

Honey Mustard Glazed Ham

Ingredients:

- 1 fully cooked bone-in ham (7-9 pounds)
- 1 cup Dijon mustard

- 1/2 cup honey
- 1/4 cup brown sugar, packed
- 2 tablespoons apple cider vinegar
- 1 teaspoon ground cloves
- 1 teaspoon ground cinnamon
- 1/2 teaspoon ground nutmeg
- Whole cloves (optional, for decoration)

Instructions:

Preheat your oven to 325°F (163°C).
Remove the ham from its packaging and place it on a roasting pan, cut side down.
In a bowl, whisk together Dijon mustard, honey, brown sugar, apple cider vinegar, ground cloves, ground cinnamon, and ground nutmeg. This will be your honey mustard glaze.
Score the surface of the ham by making shallow cuts in a diamond pattern. This helps the glaze penetrate the ham.
Brush a generous amount of the honey mustard glaze over the entire surface of the ham.
If desired, insert whole cloves into the ham's scored diamond pattern for added decoration and flavor.
Cover the ham loosely with aluminum foil and bake in the preheated oven for about 1 to 1.5 hours, or until the internal temperature reaches 140°F (60°C).
Every 30 minutes, baste the ham with the drippings in the pan and apply more honey mustard glaze.
During the last 15-20 minutes of cooking, remove the foil to allow the glaze to caramelize and create a golden-brown finish.
Once the ham reaches the desired temperature, remove it from the oven and let it rest for 15 minutes before carving.
Slice the ham and serve with any remaining honey mustard glaze as a sauce.

This Honey Mustard Glazed Ham is a festive and flavorful option for holiday dinners or special occasions. The combination of sweet honey, tangy mustard, and aromatic spices creates a deliciously glazed ham that's sure to be a hit with your guests. Enjoy the warmth and sweetness of this classic recipe!

Balsamic-Glazed Pork Loin

Ingredients:

- 2 to 2.5 pounds pork loin
- Salt and black pepper, to taste

- 3 tablespoons olive oil
- 4 cloves garlic, minced
- 1 teaspoon dried thyme
- 1 teaspoon dried rosemary
- 1/2 cup balsamic vinegar
- 1/4 cup honey
- 2 tablespoons Dijon mustard
- 1 cup chicken broth
- Fresh parsley, chopped (for garnish, optional)

Instructions:

Preheat your oven to 375°F (190°C).
Season the pork loin with salt and black pepper on all sides.
In a large oven-safe skillet, heat olive oil over medium-high heat.
Sear the pork loin on all sides until golden brown, about 2-3 minutes per side.
Remove from the skillet and set aside.
In the same skillet, add minced garlic, dried thyme, and dried rosemary. Sauté for about 1-2 minutes until fragrant.
Add balsamic vinegar, honey, and Dijon mustard to the skillet. Stir to combine and let it simmer for 2-3 minutes, allowing the flavors to meld.
Pour in the chicken broth and bring the mixture to a gentle boil.
Return the seared pork loin to the skillet, turning to coat it with the balsamic glaze.
Transfer the skillet to the preheated oven and roast for 25-30 minutes or until the internal temperature of the pork loin reaches 145°F (63°C).
Baste the pork with the glaze every 10 minutes while roasting.
Once cooked, remove the skillet from the oven and transfer the pork to a cutting board. Let it rest for 10 minutes before slicing.
Spoon the balsamic glaze from the skillet over the sliced pork loin.
Optionally, garnish with fresh chopped parsley for a burst of color and added flavor.
Serve the Balsamic-Glazed Pork Loin slices with the remaining glaze and your favorite side dishes.

This Balsamic-Glazed Pork Loin recipe results in a succulent and flavorful dish with a perfect balance of sweet and tangy notes. The balsamic glaze adds a rich and caramelized coating to the pork loin, making it an elegant and delicious option for a special dinner. Enjoy the exquisite flavors of this impressive yet easy-to-make dish!

Korean BBQ Pork Belly

Ingredients:

For the Marinade:

- 1.5 pounds pork belly, thinly sliced
- 1/4 cup soy sauce
- 2 tablespoons gochujang (Korean red pepper paste)
- 2 tablespoons mirin (or rice wine)
- 2 tablespoons honey
- 2 tablespoons sesame oil
- 4 cloves garlic, minced
- 1 tablespoon ginger, grated
- 1 tablespoon brown sugar
- 1 teaspoon black pepper

For Serving:

- Fresh lettuce leaves (for wrapping)
- Ssamjang (Korean dipping sauce)
- Thinly sliced green onions (for garnish)
- Sesame seeds (for garnish)
- Kimchi (optional)

Instructions:

In a bowl, whisk together soy sauce, gochujang, mirin, honey, sesame oil, minced garlic, grated ginger, brown sugar, and black pepper to create the marinade.
Place the thinly sliced pork belly in a shallow dish or a zip-top bag.
Pour the marinade over the pork belly, ensuring each slice is coated. Marinate in the refrigerator for at least 2 hours, or ideally overnight for maximum flavor.
Preheat a grill or grill pan over medium-high heat.
Remove the marinated pork belly from the refrigerator and let it come to room temperature for about 15 minutes.
Grill the pork slices for 2-3 minutes per side or until they are cooked through and have a nice char.
While grilling, baste the pork with any remaining marinade to enhance the flavor.
Once cooked, transfer the Korean BBQ pork belly to a serving plate.
Serve the grilled pork belly with fresh lettuce leaves for wrapping. Add a dollop of ssamjang, garnish with sliced green onions and sesame seeds.
Optionally, serve with kimchi on the side for an extra burst of flavor.

Encourage your guests to create their own wraps by placing a slice of grilled pork belly inside a lettuce leaf, adding a spoonful of ssamjang, and garnishing with green onions and sesame seeds.

This Korean BBQ Pork Belly recipe offers a delightful combination of sweet, savory, and spicy flavors. The thin slices of pork belly char beautifully on the grill, creating a mouthwatering dish that's perfect for a shared and interactive dining experience. Enjoy the authentic taste of Korean BBQ at home with this delicious recipe!

Apple Cider Braised Pork Shoulder

Ingredients:

- 4-5 pounds pork shoulder, bone-in

- Salt and black pepper, to taste
- 2 tablespoons vegetable oil
- 2 large onions, thinly sliced
- 4 cloves garlic, minced
- 2 cups apple cider
- 1 cup chicken broth
- 1/4 cup apple cider vinegar
- 1/4 cup Dijon mustard
- 1/4 cup brown sugar, packed
- 2 teaspoons dried thyme
- 2 bay leaves
- 4 large apples, peeled, cored, and sliced
- Fresh parsley, chopped (for garnish, optional)

Instructions:

Preheat your oven to 325°F (163°C).
Season the pork shoulder generously with salt and black pepper.
In a large Dutch oven or oven-safe pot, heat vegetable oil over medium-high heat.
Sear the pork shoulder on all sides until browned, about 4-5 minutes per side.
Remove the pork and set it aside.
In the same pot, add sliced onions and garlic. Sauté until the onions are softened and translucent.
Pour in the apple cider, chicken broth, apple cider vinegar, Dijon mustard, brown sugar, dried thyme, and add the bay leaves. Stir to combine.
Return the seared pork shoulder to the pot, ensuring it is partially submerged in the liquid.
Bring the liquid to a simmer, then cover the pot and transfer it to the preheated oven.
Braise the pork in the oven for 3 to 3.5 hours or until the meat is tender and easily pulls apart.
About 30 minutes before the end of the cooking time, add the sliced apples to the pot, allowing them to cook in the flavorful liquid.
Once cooked, remove the pot from the oven and discard the bay leaves.
Using two forks, shred the pork directly in the pot, mixing it with the apples and the braising liquid.
Serve the apple cider braised pork shoulder over your favorite side dishes, garnished with fresh chopped parsley if desired.

This Apple Cider Braised Pork Shoulder recipe results in a succulent and flavorful dish with the sweetness of apple cider complementing the richness of the pork. Perfect for a cozy family dinner or a festive occasion, this braised pork shoulder will fill your kitchen with irresistible aromas and satisfy your taste buds with every tender bite. Enjoy the comforting flavors of this delicious dish!

Teriyaki Pork Stir-Fry

Ingredients:

For the Pork Marinade:

- 1 pound pork tenderloin, thinly sliced
- 2 tablespoons soy sauce
- 2 tablespoons mirin (sweet rice wine)
- 1 tablespoon sake (or white wine)
- 1 tablespoon brown sugar
- 1 teaspoon sesame oil
- 2 cloves garlic, minced
- 1 teaspoon ginger, grated

For the Stir-Fry:

- 2 tablespoons vegetable oil
- 1 red bell pepper, thinly sliced
- 1 yellow bell pepper, thinly sliced
- 1 cup broccoli florets
- 1 carrot, julienned
- 1 cup snap peas, ends trimmed
- 3 green onions, sliced
- Sesame seeds, for garnish (optional)
- Cooked rice, for serving

For the Teriyaki Sauce:

- 1/4 cup soy sauce
- 2 tablespoons mirin
- 1 tablespoon sake (or white wine)
- 2 tablespoons brown sugar
- 1 teaspoon sesame oil

Instructions:

In a bowl, combine the pork marinade ingredients: soy sauce, mirin, sake, brown sugar, sesame oil, minced garlic, and grated ginger. Add the thinly sliced pork and let it marinate for at least 20 minutes.

In a small bowl, mix together the teriyaki sauce ingredients: soy sauce, mirin, sake, brown sugar, and sesame oil. Set aside.

Heat vegetable oil in a wok or large skillet over medium-high heat.

Stir-fry the marinated pork slices until browned and cooked through. Remove the pork from the wok and set it aside.
In the same wok, add a bit more oil if needed and stir-fry the bell peppers, broccoli, carrot, and snap peas until crisp-tender.
Add the cooked pork back to the wok along with the sliced green onions.
Pour the teriyaki sauce over the stir-fry and toss everything together until well-coated and heated through.
Serve the teriyaki pork stir-fry over cooked rice.
Garnish with sesame seeds if desired.

This Teriyaki Pork Stir-Fry is a quick and flavorful dish that brings the perfect balance of savory and sweet. The marinated pork combined with colorful vegetables and a homemade teriyaki sauce creates a delicious and satisfying meal. Enjoy this stir-fry over a bed of rice for a complete and delightful dining experience!

Cajun Spiced Pork Ribs

Ingredients:

For the Cajun Spice Rub:

- 2 tablespoons paprika
- 1 tablespoon onion powder
- 1 tablespoon garlic powder
- 1 tablespoon dried thyme
- 1 tablespoon dried oregano
- 1 tablespoon brown sugar
- 1 teaspoon cayenne pepper (adjust to taste)
- 1 teaspoon black pepper
- 1 teaspoon white pepper
- 1 teaspoon smoked paprika
- 1 teaspoon salt

For the Pork Ribs:

- 2 racks of pork ribs (baby back or spare ribs)
- 2 tablespoons olive oil
- 4 cloves garlic, minced
- 1 cup chicken broth
- 1/4 cup apple cider vinegar
- 1/4 cup Worcestershire sauce
- 1/4 cup tomato paste
- 1 tablespoon Dijon mustard
- 2 tablespoons honey

Instructions:

Preheat your oven to 300°F (150°C).
In a bowl, combine all the ingredients for the Cajun spice rub. Mix well.
Pat the pork ribs dry with paper towels. Rub the Cajun spice mixture evenly over both sides of the ribs.
In a large oven-safe pot or Dutch oven, heat olive oil over medium-high heat.
Sear the ribs on both sides until browned, about 3-4 minutes per side. Remove the ribs and set them aside.
In the same pot, add minced garlic and sauté until fragrant.
Pour in the chicken broth, apple cider vinegar, Worcestershire sauce, tomato paste, Dijon mustard, and honey. Stir to combine and bring to a simmer.

Return the seared ribs to the pot, ensuring they are partially submerged in the liquid.
Cover the pot with a lid or aluminum foil and transfer it to the preheated oven.
Braise the ribs in the oven for 2.5 to 3 hours or until the meat is tender and easily pulls away from the bones.
Every 30 minutes, baste the ribs with the cooking liquid.
Optional: Finish the ribs on a preheated grill or under the broiler for a few minutes to add a smoky char.
Once cooked, remove the ribs from the oven and let them rest for 10 minutes before slicing.
Serve the Cajun Spiced Pork Ribs with the cooking liquid as a dipping sauce.

These Cajun Spiced Pork Ribs are a flavor-packed delight, combining the bold and aromatic Cajun spice rub with the tenderness of slow-cooked ribs. Whether enjoyed for a casual weeknight meal or a festive gathering, these ribs are sure to satisfy your craving for a delicious and spicy barbecue experience. Get ready to savor every bite!

Cuban Mojo Pork

Ingredients:

For the Marinade:

- 4-5 pounds pork shoulder, bone-in
- 1 cup orange juice
- 1/2 cup lime juice
- 1/4 cup lemon juice
- 6 cloves garlic, minced
- 1 teaspoon cumin
- 1 teaspoon dried oregano
- 1 teaspoon smoked paprika
- 1 teaspoon ground coriander
- 1 teaspoon salt
- 1/2 teaspoon black pepper
- 1/2 cup fresh cilantro, chopped

For Cooking:

- 2 tablespoons olive oil
- 1 onion, thinly sliced
- 1 cup chicken broth

Instructions:

In a bowl, combine orange juice, lime juice, lemon juice, minced garlic, cumin, oregano, smoked paprika, ground coriander, salt, black pepper, and chopped cilantro to create the marinade.

Place the pork shoulder in a large resealable plastic bag or a marinating dish. Pour the marinade over the pork, making sure it is well-coated. Seal the bag or cover the dish and refrigerate for at least 4 hours, preferably overnight.

Preheat your oven to 325°F (163°C).

Remove the pork from the refrigerator and let it come to room temperature for about 30 minutes.

Heat olive oil in a large Dutch oven or oven-safe pot over medium-high heat.

Sear the pork shoulder on all sides until browned, about 4-5 minutes per side. Remove the pork and set it aside.

In the same pot, add sliced onions and sauté until softened.

Place the seared pork shoulder back into the pot. Pour in the chicken broth.

Cover the pot with a lid and transfer it to the preheated oven.

Braise the pork in the oven for 3 to 3.5 hours or until the meat is fork-tender and easily pulls apart.

Optional: For a crispy exterior, you can place the cooked pork under the broiler for a few minutes.

Once cooked, remove the pot from the oven and let the pork rest for 10-15 minutes.

Shred the pork using two forks and mix it with the onions and cooking liquid.

Serve the Cuban Mojo Pork over rice, with black beans, or in Cuban sandwiches.

This Cuban Mojo Pork is a celebration of citrusy and garlicky flavors, creating a succulent and aromatic dish that captures the essence of Cuban cuisine. Whether served as a main dish or used in sandwiches, the slow-marinated and slow-cooked pork promises a mouthwatering experience. Enjoy the vibrant and delicious taste of this Cuban classic!

Mediterranean Stuffed Pork Loin

Ingredients:

For the Pork Loin:

- 2 to 2.5 pounds pork loin, butterflied
- Salt and black pepper, to taste
- 2 tablespoons olive oil

For the Mediterranean Stuffing:

- 1 cup baby spinach, chopped
- 1/2 cup sun-dried tomatoes, chopped
- 1/2 cup Kalamata olives, pitted and chopped
- 1/2 cup feta cheese, crumbled
- 3 cloves garlic, minced
- 1 tablespoon fresh rosemary, chopped
- 1 tablespoon fresh thyme, chopped
- Zest of 1 lemon
- Salt and black pepper, to taste

For Roasting:

- 1 tablespoon Dijon mustard
- 1 tablespoon balsamic glaze (optional, for drizzling)
- Kitchen twine for tying

Instructions:

Preheat your oven to 375°F (190°C).
Butterfly the pork loin by making a lengthwise cut along the center, but not cutting through. Open it like a book and flatten with a meat mallet if necessary.
Season the inside of the butterflied pork loin with salt and black pepper.
In a bowl, combine chopped baby spinach, sun-dried tomatoes, Kalamata olives, crumbled feta cheese, minced garlic, fresh rosemary, fresh thyme, and lemon zest. Mix well to create the Mediterranean stuffing.
Spread the Mediterranean stuffing evenly over the inside of the butterflied pork loin.
Carefully roll the pork loin back together, making sure the stuffing is enclosed. Tie the rolled pork loin with kitchen twine at intervals to secure it.
Rub the outside of the pork loin with olive oil, salt, and black pepper.
Place the stuffed and tied pork loin on a roasting pan or oven-safe skillet.

Brush the surface of the pork loin with Dijon mustard.
Roast in the preheated oven for approximately 60-70 minutes or until the internal temperature reaches 145°F (63°C).
Optionally, drizzle balsamic glaze over the pork loin during the last 10 minutes of cooking for a flavorful glaze.
Once cooked, remove the pork loin from the oven and let it rest for 10-15 minutes.
Slice the Mediterranean Stuffed Pork Loin into rounds and serve.

This Mediterranean Stuffed Pork Loin is a show-stopping dish that combines the savory and tangy flavors of the Mediterranean. The butterflied pork loin is filled with a vibrant mixture of spinach, sun-dried tomatoes, olives, feta, and aromatic herbs, creating a delightful fusion of tastes. Whether for a special occasion or a family dinner, this stuffed pork loin will impress with its flavors and presentation. Enjoy the taste of the Mediterranean with every bite!

Pineapple and Soy-Glazed Pork Chops

Ingredients:

For the Marinade:

- 4 bone-in pork chops
- 1 cup pineapple juice
- 1/4 cup soy sauce
- 2 tablespoons honey
- 2 tablespoons rice vinegar
- 2 cloves garlic, minced
- 1 teaspoon ginger, grated
- 1/2 teaspoon red pepper flakes (optional, for heat)
- Salt and black pepper, to taste

For Cooking:

- 2 tablespoons vegetable oil
- Pineapple slices (fresh or canned), for garnish
- Green onions, chopped (for garnish, optional)
- Sesame seeds, for garnish (optional)

Instructions:

In a bowl, whisk together pineapple juice, soy sauce, honey, rice vinegar, minced garlic, grated ginger, red pepper flakes (if using), salt, and black pepper to create the marinade.
Place the pork chops in a resealable plastic bag or a shallow dish. Pour the marinade over the pork chops, ensuring they are well-coated. Seal the bag or cover the dish and refrigerate for at least 30 minutes, allowing the flavors to infuse.
Preheat your oven to 375°F (190°C).
Heat vegetable oil in an oven-safe skillet over medium-high heat.
Remove the pork chops from the marinade, letting excess marinade drip off.
Sear the pork chops for 2-3 minutes per side until browned.
Pour the remaining marinade into the skillet and bring it to a simmer.
Place the skillet in the preheated oven and roast for about 15-20 minutes or until the internal temperature of the pork chops reaches 145°F (63°C).
During the last few minutes of cooking, add pineapple slices to the skillet, allowing them to caramelize.

Optional: For additional color and flavor, you can broil the pork chops for a couple of minutes.

Once cooked, remove the skillet from the oven.

Serve the Pineapple and Soy-Glazed Pork Chops over rice or your favorite side dish.

Garnish with caramelized pineapple slices, chopped green onions, and sesame seeds if desired.

These Pineapple and Soy-Glazed Pork Chops offer a delightful combination of sweet and savory flavors. The marinade infuses the pork chops with the tropical taste of pineapple and the umami richness of soy sauce. The caramelized pineapple slices add a touch of sweetness to the dish, creating a well-balanced and delicious meal. Enjoy this easy-to-make recipe for a quick and flavorful dinner!

Thai Basil Pork Stir-Fry

Ingredients:

- 1 pound pork tenderloin, thinly sliced
- 2 tablespoons vegetable oil
- 4 cloves garlic, minced
- 1 red chili, thinly sliced (adjust to spice preference)
- 1 bell pepper, thinly sliced
- 1 onion, thinly sliced
- 1 cup Thai basil leaves, loosely packed
- 2 tablespoons oyster sauce
- 1 tablespoon soy sauce
- 1 tablespoon fish sauce
- 1 teaspoon sugar
- Lime wedges, for serving
- Cooked jasmine rice, for serving

Instructions:

Heat vegetable oil in a wok or a large skillet over medium-high heat.
Add minced garlic and sliced pork to the hot oil. Stir-fry until the pork is browned and cooked through.
Add sliced red chili, bell pepper, and onion to the wok. Continue stir-frying for 2-3 minutes until the vegetables are slightly tender.
In a small bowl, mix together oyster sauce, soy sauce, fish sauce, and sugar.
Pour the sauce mixture over the pork and vegetables. Toss everything together to ensure even coating.
Add Thai basil leaves to the stir-fry and toss until the basil is just wilted.
Taste and adjust the seasoning if needed. You can add more soy sauce, fish sauce, or sugar according to your preference.
Remove the wok from heat.
Serve the Thai Basil Pork Stir-Fry over cooked jasmine rice.
Garnish with additional Thai basil leaves and lime wedges on the side.

This Thai Basil Pork Stir-Fry is a quick and flavorful dish that combines the aromatic Thai basil with a savory and slightly spicy sauce. It's a perfect balance of sweet, salty, and umami flavors, creating a delicious and satisfying meal. Enjoy the vibrant and authentic taste of Thai cuisine in the comfort of your own kitchen!

Beer-Braised Bratwurst

Ingredients:

- 4 bratwurst sausages
- 2 tablespoons vegetable oil
- 1 onion, thinly sliced
- 2 cloves garlic, minced
- 1 bottle (12 ounces) beer (such as a lager or pilsner)
- 1 cup chicken or vegetable broth
- 2 tablespoons Dijon mustard
- 1 tablespoon whole grain mustard
- 1 tablespoon brown sugar
- Salt and black pepper, to taste
- Fresh parsley, chopped (for garnish, optional)
- Bratwurst buns or rolls, for serving

Instructions:

In a large skillet or a Dutch oven, heat vegetable oil over medium-high heat.
Brown the bratwurst sausages on all sides, about 4-5 minutes.
Add thinly sliced onions to the skillet and sauté until they become translucent.
Stir in minced garlic and cook for an additional 1-2 minutes until fragrant.
Pour in the beer and chicken or vegetable broth, ensuring the bratwurst sausages are partially submerged.
Add Dijon mustard, whole grain mustard, and brown sugar to the liquid. Stir to combine.
Season with salt and black pepper to taste.
Bring the liquid to a simmer, then reduce the heat to low. Cover the skillet and let it simmer for about 20-25 minutes or until the bratwursts are fully cooked.
Optional: If you prefer a grilled finish, you can transfer the bratwursts to a hot grill for a few minutes after braising.
Remove the bratwursts from the skillet.
Optionally, continue simmering the liquid until it reduces to a thicker consistency.
Serve the bratwursts in buns or rolls, topped with the beer-braised onions and a drizzle of the reduced sauce.
Garnish with chopped fresh parsley if desired.

Enjoy these Beer-Braised Bratwursts, infused with the rich flavors of beer, mustard, and onions. This recipe delivers a delicious and hearty meal, perfect for gatherings or a comforting weeknight dinner. Serve with your favorite sides and perhaps some additional mustard for dipping. Cheers to a tasty and satisfying dish!

Peach and Bourbon Glazed Pork Tenderloin

Ingredients:

For the Pork Tenderloin:

- 2 pork tenderloins (about 1 pound each)
- Salt and black pepper, to taste
- 2 tablespoons olive oil

For the Peach and Bourbon Glaze:

- 1 cup fresh or frozen peaches, chopped
- 1/4 cup bourbon
- 1/4 cup brown sugar
- 2 tablespoons Dijon mustard
- 2 tablespoons soy sauce
- 1 tablespoon apple cider vinegar
- 2 cloves garlic, minced
- 1 teaspoon fresh ginger, grated
- 1/4 teaspoon red pepper flakes (optional, for heat)

Instructions:

Preheat your oven to 375°F (190°C).
Season the pork tenderloins with salt and black pepper on all sides.
In a large oven-safe skillet, heat olive oil over medium-high heat.
Sear the pork tenderloins on all sides until browned, about 2-3 minutes per side.
While the pork is searing, prepare the glaze. In a blender or food processor, combine chopped peaches, bourbon, brown sugar, Dijon mustard, soy sauce, apple cider vinegar, minced garlic, grated ginger, and red pepper flakes (if using). Blend until smooth.
Once the pork is seared, pour the peach and bourbon glaze over the tenderloins.
Transfer the skillet to the preheated oven and roast for about 15-20 minutes or until the internal temperature of the pork reaches 145°F (63°C), basting with the glaze halfway through.
Remove the skillet from the oven and let the pork rest for a few minutes.
Slice the pork tenderloins and serve with the peach and bourbon glaze drizzled over the top.
Optionally, garnish with fresh peach slices and chopped herbs for added freshness.

This Peach and Bourbon Glazed Pork Tenderloin is a delightful combination of sweet and savory flavors, making it a perfect choice for a special dinner. The peach and bourbon glaze adds a luscious and aromatic touch to the tender pork. Serve this dish with your favorite side dishes for a complete and impressive meal. Enjoy the delicious harmony of flavors!

Italian Sausage and Peppers

Ingredients:

- 1.5 lbs Italian sausage links (sweet or hot), cut into 3-inch pieces
- 2 tablespoons olive oil
- 1 large onion, thinly sliced
- 3 bell peppers (assorted colors), thinly sliced
- 4 cloves garlic, minced
- 1 can (14 ounces) crushed tomatoes
- 1 teaspoon dried oregano
- 1 teaspoon dried basil
- 1/2 teaspoon red pepper flakes (optional, for heat)
- Salt and black pepper, to taste
- Fresh parsley, chopped (for garnish)
- Sub rolls or Italian bread, for serving

Instructions:

In a large skillet or Dutch oven, heat olive oil over medium-high heat.
Add the Italian sausage pieces to the skillet and brown them on all sides, about 5-7 minutes. Ensure the sausage is cooked through.
Remove the browned sausage from the skillet and set it aside.
In the same skillet, add sliced onions and bell peppers. Sauté until they are softened and slightly caramelized, about 5-7 minutes.
Add minced garlic to the skillet and sauté for an additional 1-2 minutes until fragrant.
Pour in the crushed tomatoes, dried oregano, dried basil, and red pepper flakes (if using). Stir to combine.
Return the browned sausage to the skillet, nestling it into the pepper and onion mixture.
Season the dish with salt and black pepper to taste. Stir gently to coat the sausage, peppers, and onions with the tomato mixture.
Cover the skillet and let it simmer over medium-low heat for about 20-25 minutes, allowing the flavors to meld.
Optional: For a thicker sauce, uncover the skillet and simmer for an additional 10-15 minutes.
Garnish with chopped fresh parsley.
Serve the Italian Sausage and Peppers in sub rolls or over Italian bread.

This classic Italian Sausage and Peppers dish is a hearty and flavorful meal that is perfect for gatherings or a satisfying weeknight dinner. The combination of sweet or hot

Italian sausage with colorful bell peppers and onions creates a deliciously savory experience. Enjoy this comforting and timeless Italian-American favorite!

Jamaican Jerk Pork

Ingredients:

For the Jerk Marinade:

- 3 green onions, chopped
- 4-5 sprigs fresh thyme, leaves only
- 2 Scotch bonnet peppers, seeds removed and chopped
- 4 cloves garlic, minced
- 1 tablespoon ginger, grated
- 1 tablespoon ground allspice
- 1 tablespoon ground cinnamon
- 1 tablespoon ground nutmeg
- 1 tablespoon ground black pepper
- 2 tablespoons soy sauce
- 2 tablespoons vegetable oil
- 1 tablespoon brown sugar
- Juice of 2 limes
- 2 tablespoons apple cider vinegar
- 2 teaspoons salt

For the Pork:

- 3-4 pounds pork shoulder, cut into large chunks or strips
- 2 tablespoons vegetable oil (for grilling or roasting)

Instructions:

In a blender or food processor, combine all the jerk marinade ingredients. Blend until you have a smooth paste.
Place the pork chunks or strips in a large bowl or a resealable plastic bag.
Coat the pork with the jerk marinade, ensuring each piece is well covered. If using a bag, seal it, removing excess air, and massage the marinade into the meat.
Marinate the pork in the refrigerator for at least 4 hours, or ideally overnight, to allow the flavors to penetrate the meat.
Preheat your grill or oven to medium-high heat.
If using a grill, brush the grates with oil to prevent sticking.
Remove the marinated pork from the refrigerator and let it come to room temperature for about 30 minutes.
Thread the pork onto skewers or place the pieces directly on the grill.

Grill the pork for about 15-20 minutes, turning occasionally, until it reaches an internal temperature of 145°F (63°C) and has a nice char.

If using an oven, preheat to 375°F (190°C). Place the pork on a roasting rack set over a baking sheet and roast for 45-60 minutes or until cooked through, turning once for even cooking.

Allow the Jamaican Jerk Pork to rest for a few minutes before serving.

Serve with traditional sides like rice and peas, coleslaw, or fried plantains.

This Jamaican Jerk Pork recipe delivers the bold and fiery flavors characteristic of Jamaican cuisine. The jerk marinade, rich in aromatic spices and heat from Scotch bonnet peppers, imparts a distinctive taste to the succulent pork. Whether grilled or roasted, this dish promises a delicious and spicy culinary adventure. Enjoy the vibrant and authentic flavors of Jamaica with this Jamaican Jerk Pork!

Mustard and Brown Sugar Glazed Ham

Ingredients:

- 1 bone-in ham, fully cooked (7-9 pounds)
- 1 cup Dijon mustard
- 1 cup brown sugar, packed
- 1/4 cup apple cider vinegar
- 2 tablespoons whole grain mustard
- 1 teaspoon garlic powder
- 1 teaspoon onion powder
- 1/2 teaspoon black pepper
- 1/4 teaspoon ground cloves (optional, for a hint of spice)
- Whole cloves (for decoration, optional)

Instructions:

Preheat your oven to 325°F (163°C).

Remove the ham from its packaging and place it on a roasting pan, cut side down.

In a bowl, whisk together Dijon mustard, brown sugar, apple cider vinegar, whole grain mustard, garlic powder, onion powder, black pepper, and ground cloves (if using). This will be your glaze.

Score the surface of the ham by making shallow cuts in a diamond pattern. This helps the glaze penetrate the ham.

Brush a generous amount of the mustard and brown sugar glaze over the entire surface of the ham.

If desired, insert whole cloves into the ham's scored diamond pattern for added decoration and flavor.

Cover the ham loosely with aluminum foil and bake in the preheated oven for about 1 to 1.5 hours, or until the internal temperature reaches 140°F (60°C).

Every 30 minutes, baste the ham with the drippings in the pan and apply more glaze.

During the last 15-20 minutes of cooking, remove the foil to allow the glaze to caramelize and create a golden-brown finish.

Once the ham reaches the desired temperature, remove it from the oven and let it rest for 15 minutes before carving.

Slice the ham and serve with any remaining glaze as a sauce.

This Mustard and Brown Sugar Glazed Ham is a delightful combination of sweet, tangy, and savory flavors that create a mouthwatering and festive centerpiece for special occasions or holiday gatherings. The glaze caramelizes beautifully, adding a rich and flavorful coating to the succulent ham. Enjoy the savory-sweet goodness of this classic glazed ham!

Szechuan-style Shredded Pork

Ingredients:

For the Marinade:

- 1 pound pork tenderloin, thinly sliced into strips
- 2 tablespoons soy sauce
- 1 tablespoon Shaoxing wine (Chinese rice wine) or dry sherry
- 1 tablespoon cornstarch
- 1 teaspoon sesame oil
- 1 teaspoon sugar

For the Sauce:

- 2 tablespoons soy sauce
- 1 tablespoon hoisin sauce
- 1 tablespoon black vinegar
- 1 tablespoon oyster sauce
- 1 tablespoon water
- 1 teaspoon sugar
- 1 teaspoon cornstarch

For Stir-Frying:

- 2 tablespoons vegetable oil
- 3 cloves garlic, minced
- 1 tablespoon ginger, grated
- 2-3 red chili peppers, thinly sliced (adjust to spice preference)
- 1 cup shredded cabbage
- 1 cup julienned carrots
- 1/2 cup sliced green onions (scallions)
- 1/4 cup chopped peanuts (for garnish, optional)
- Cooked white rice, for serving

Instructions:

In a bowl, mix the pork slices with soy sauce, Shaoxing wine, cornstarch, sesame oil, and sugar. Allow it to marinate for at least 20 minutes.

In a small bowl, combine the ingredients for the sauce: soy sauce, hoisin sauce, black vinegar, oyster sauce, water, sugar, and cornstarch. Stir until the cornstarch is dissolved.

Heat vegetable oil in a wok or a large skillet over high heat.

Add the marinated pork slices to the hot oil. Stir-fry for 2-3 minutes or until the pork is cooked through and slightly caramelized. Remove the pork from the wok and set it aside.

In the same wok, add a bit more oil if needed. Add minced garlic, grated ginger, and sliced red chili peppers. Stir-fry for about 30 seconds until fragrant.

Add shredded cabbage and julienned carrots to the wok. Stir-fry for 2-3 minutes until the vegetables are crisp-tender.

Return the cooked pork to the wok.

Pour the prepared sauce over the pork and vegetables. Toss everything together until well-coated and heated through.

Add sliced green onions and toss for an additional minute.

Optional: Garnish with chopped peanuts for added crunch.

Serve the Szechuan-style Shredded Pork over cooked white rice.

This Szechuan-style Shredded Pork recipe delivers a flavorful and spicy stir-fry that captures the essence of Szechuan cuisine. The combination of marinated pork, crisp vegetables, and a bold, savory sauce creates a delicious and satisfying dish. Enjoy the aromatic and spicy flavors of this Chinese-inspired stir-fry served over a bed of fluffy white rice!

Apricot Glazed Pork Loin

Ingredients:

For the Pork Loin:

- 2 to 2.5 pounds pork loin
- Salt and black pepper, to taste
- 2 tablespoons olive oil

For the Apricot Glaze:

- 1 cup apricot preserves
- 2 tablespoons Dijon mustard
- 2 tablespoons soy sauce
- 2 tablespoons apple cider vinegar
- 2 cloves garlic, minced
- 1 teaspoon fresh ginger, grated
- 1/2 teaspoon red pepper flakes (optional, for heat)

Instructions:

Preheat your oven to 375°F (190°C).
Season the pork loin with salt and black pepper on all sides.
In a large oven-safe skillet, heat olive oil over medium-high heat.
Sear the pork loin on all sides until browned, about 2-3 minutes per side.
While the pork is searing, prepare the apricot glaze. In a small saucepan, combine apricot preserves, Dijon mustard, soy sauce, apple cider vinegar, minced garlic, grated ginger, and red pepper flakes (if using). Heat over medium heat, stirring until the preserves are melted and the ingredients are well combined. Remove from heat.
Brush a generous amount of the apricot glaze over the entire surface of the seared pork loin.
Transfer the skillet to the preheated oven and roast for about 25-30 minutes or until the internal temperature of the pork loin reaches 145°F (63°C).
Baste the pork loin with the apricot glaze every 10 minutes during the roasting process.
Optional: For a caramelized finish, you can broil the pork loin for a few minutes after roasting.
Once cooked, remove the skillet from the oven and let the pork loin rest for 10 minutes.

Slice the Apricot Glazed Pork Loin into rounds and serve with any remaining glaze.

This Apricot Glazed Pork Loin recipe offers a delightful combination of sweet and tangy flavors that enhance the natural richness of the pork. The apricot glaze creates a glossy and flavorful coating, making it a perfect choice for a special dinner or festive occasion. Enjoy the succulent and aromatic taste of this apricot-infused dish!

Chipotle Lime Pork Tacos

Ingredients:

For the Chipotle Lime Marinade:

- 2 pounds pork shoulder or pork butt, cut into chunks
- 2 chipotle peppers in adobo sauce, chopped
- 3 tablespoons adobo sauce (from the chipotle peppers can)
- 3 cloves garlic, minced
- 2 tablespoons olive oil
- Juice of 2 limes
- 1 tablespoon ground cumin
- 1 tablespoon dried oregano
- 1 teaspoon smoked paprika
- 1 teaspoon onion powder
- Salt and black pepper, to taste

For Assembling Tacos:

- Corn or flour tortillas
- Shredded lettuce or cabbage
- Diced tomatoes
- Sliced red onions
- Fresh cilantro, chopped
- Crumbled feta or queso fresco
- Lime wedges for serving

Instructions:

In a blender or food processor, combine all the chipotle lime marinade ingredients: chipotle peppers, adobo sauce, minced garlic, olive oil, lime juice, ground cumin, dried oregano, smoked paprika, onion powder, salt, and black pepper. Blend until you have a smooth marinade.
Place the pork chunks in a large bowl or a resealable plastic bag.
Pour the chipotle lime marinade over the pork, ensuring each piece is well coated. If using a bag, seal it, removing excess air, and massage the marinade into the meat.
Marinate the pork in the refrigerator for at least 4 hours, or ideally overnight, to allow the flavors to penetrate the meat.
Preheat your grill or grill pan to medium-high heat.
Remove the marinated pork from the refrigerator and let it come to room temperature for about 30 minutes.

Thread the pork onto skewers or place the pieces directly on the grill.
Grill the pork for about 15-20 minutes, turning occasionally, until it reaches an internal temperature of 145°F (63°C) and has a nice char.
While the pork is grilling, warm the tortillas on the grill for about 30 seconds on each side.
Remove the pork from the grill and let it rest for a few minutes.
Assemble the tacos by placing some grilled pork in each tortilla.
Top with shredded lettuce or cabbage, diced tomatoes, sliced red onions, fresh cilantro, and crumbled feta or queso fresco.
Serve the Chipotle Lime Pork Tacos with lime wedges on the side.

These Chipotle Lime Pork Tacos are bursting with bold and zesty flavors, making them a perfect choice for a flavorful taco night. The chipotle-infused marinade adds a smoky kick, complemented by the brightness of lime juice. Customize your tacos with your favorite toppings for a delicious and satisfying meal. Enjoy the delicious fusion of smoky, spicy, and citrusy notes in every bite!

Cider-Braised Pork Belly

Ingredients:

- 2 pounds pork belly, skin-on, cut into chunks
- Salt and black pepper, to taste
- 2 tablespoons vegetable oil
- 1 onion, chopped
- 2 carrots, chopped
- 3 cloves garlic, minced
- 2 cups apple cider
- 1 cup chicken or vegetable broth
- 2 tablespoons Dijon mustard
- 2 tablespoons maple syrup
- 2 bay leaves
- Fresh thyme sprigs, for garnish

Instructions:

Preheat your oven to 325°F (163°C).
Season the pork belly chunks with salt and black pepper.
Heat vegetable oil in a large oven-safe Dutch oven or skillet over medium-high heat.
Brown the pork belly chunks on all sides, working in batches if necessary.
Remove the browned pork belly from the pot and set it aside.
In the same pot, add chopped onion and carrots. Sauté until the vegetables are softened, about 5 minutes.
Add minced garlic to the pot and sauté for an additional 1-2 minutes until fragrant.
Pour in apple cider and chicken or vegetable broth, scraping the bottom of the pot to release any browned bits.
Stir in Dijon mustard and maple syrup.
Return the browned pork belly chunks to the pot.
Add bay leaves to the pot.
Bring the liquid to a simmer, then cover the pot with a lid.
Transfer the pot to the preheated oven and braise for about 2.5 to 3 hours, or until the pork belly is tender and easily pierced with a fork.
Remove the pot from the oven and discard the bay leaves.
Optional: For a crispy exterior, you can place the pot under the broiler for a few minutes.
Garnish the Cider-Braised Pork Belly with fresh thyme sprigs.
Serve the pork belly over mashed potatoes, polenta, or your preferred side dish.

This Cider-Braised Pork Belly recipe results in tender and succulent chunks of pork with a flavorful, cider-infused sauce. The combination of apple cider, Dijon mustard, and maple syrup creates a sweet and savory profile, while the slow braising process ensures a melt-in-your-mouth texture. Enjoy the rich and comforting taste of this cider-braised delight, perfect for a cozy dinner at home!

Filipino Adobo Pork

Ingredients:

- 2 pounds pork belly or pork shoulder, cut into chunks
- 1 onion, peeled and sliced thinly
- 5 cloves garlic, minced
- 1/2 cup soy sauce
- 1/4 cup vinegar (white or cane vinegar)
- 1 cup water
- 1 teaspoon whole peppercorns
- 3 bay leaves
- 1 tablespoon cooking oil
- Salt and pepper, to taste
- Green onions or cilantro for garnish (optional)
- Steamed rice, for serving

Instructions:

In a large bowl, combine the pork chunks, sliced onions, minced garlic, soy sauce, vinegar, water, whole peppercorns, and bay leaves. Marinate the pork in this mixture for at least 30 minutes, or preferably overnight in the refrigerator.
In a large pot or Dutch oven, heat cooking oil over medium-high heat.
Remove the pork chunks from the marinade, reserving the liquid.
Sear the pork pieces in the hot oil until browned on all sides.
Pour in the reserved marinade liquid into the pot.
Bring the mixture to a boil, then reduce the heat to low, cover, and simmer for about 45 minutes to 1 hour, or until the pork is tender.
Once the pork is tender, uncover the pot and allow the sauce to reduce and thicken for an additional 10-15 minutes.
Taste and adjust the seasoning with salt and pepper if needed.
Optional: For a caramelized finish, you can transfer the pork to a hot grill or oven and broil for a few minutes.
Garnish with chopped green onions or cilantro, if desired.
Serve the Filipino Adobo Pork over steamed rice.

This Filipino Adobo Pork recipe showcases the classic and beloved flavors of Filipino cuisine. The combination of soy sauce, vinegar, garlic, and aromatic spices creates a savory and slightly tangy dish with tender and succulent pork. Enjoy the rich and comforting taste of Filipino Adobo Pork served over a bed of steamed rice for a hearty and satisfying meal!

Filipino Adobo Pork

Ingredients:

- 2 pounds pork belly or pork shoulder, cut into chunks
- 1 onion, peeled and sliced thinly
- 5 cloves garlic, minced
- 1/2 cup soy sauce
- 1/4 cup vinegar (white or cane vinegar)
- 1 cup water
- 1 teaspoon whole peppercorns
- 3 bay leaves
- 1 tablespoon cooking oil
- Salt and pepper, to taste
- Green onions or cilantro for garnish (optional)
- Steamed rice, for serving

Instructions:

In a large bowl, combine the pork chunks, sliced onions, minced garlic, soy sauce, vinegar, water, whole peppercorns, and bay leaves. Marinate the pork in this mixture for at least 30 minutes, or preferably overnight in the refrigerator.
In a large pot or Dutch oven, heat cooking oil over medium-high heat.
Remove the pork chunks from the marinade, reserving the liquid.
Sear the pork pieces in the hot oil until browned on all sides.
Pour in the reserved marinade liquid into the pot.
Bring the mixture to a boil, then reduce the heat to low, cover, and simmer for about 45 minutes to 1 hour, or until the pork is tender.
Once the pork is tender, uncover the pot and allow the sauce to reduce and thicken for an additional 10-15 minutes.
Taste and adjust the seasoning with salt and pepper if needed.
Optional: For a caramelized finish, you can transfer the pork to a hot grill or oven and broil for a few minutes.
Garnish with chopped green onions or cilantro, if desired.
Serve the Filipino Adobo Pork over steamed rice.

This Filipino Adobo Pork recipe showcases the classic and beloved flavors of Filipino cuisine. The combination of soy sauce, vinegar, garlic, and aromatic spices creates a savory and slightly tangy dish with tender and succulent pork. Enjoy the rich and comforting taste of Filipino Adobo Pork served over a bed of steamed rice for a hearty and satisfying meal!

Cranberry and Dijon Pork Roast

Ingredients:

For the Pork Roast:

- 3-4 pounds pork loin roast
- Salt and black pepper, to taste
- 2 tablespoons olive oil

For the Cranberry and Dijon Glaze:

- 1 cup cranberry sauce (homemade or canned)
- 3 tablespoons Dijon mustard
- 2 tablespoons balsamic vinegar
- 2 tablespoons honey
- 2 cloves garlic, minced
- 1 teaspoon dried thyme (or 1 tablespoon fresh thyme leaves)

Instructions:

Preheat your oven to 375°F (190°C).
Season the pork loin roast with salt and black pepper on all sides.
In a large oven-safe skillet or roasting pan, heat olive oil over medium-high heat.
Sear the pork roast on all sides until browned, about 2-3 minutes per side.
While the pork is searing, prepare the cranberry and Dijon glaze. In a bowl, whisk together cranberry sauce, Dijon mustard, balsamic vinegar, honey, minced garlic, and dried thyme.
Once the pork is browned, pour the cranberry and Dijon glaze over the pork, ensuring it's evenly coated.
Transfer the skillet or roasting pan to the preheated oven.
Roast the pork in the oven for about 25-30 minutes per pound or until the internal temperature reaches 145°F (63°C), basting with the glaze every 15 minutes.
Optional: For a caramelized finish, you can broil the pork for a few minutes after roasting.
Remove the pork from the oven and let it rest for 10-15 minutes before slicing.
Slice the Cranberry and Dijon Pork Roast and serve with any remaining glaze.
Garnish with additional thyme leaves if desired.

This Cranberry and Dijon Pork Roast recipe offers a delightful combination of sweet and tangy flavors that complement the succulence of the pork. The cranberry and Dijon glaze adds a festive touch, making it a perfect choice for holiday dinners or special occasions. Enjoy the delicious harmony of flavors in each juicy slice of this roast!

Hoisin and Ginger Pork Skewers

Ingredients:

For the Marinade:

- 1.5 pounds pork tenderloin, cut into 1-inch cubes
- 1/4 cup hoisin sauce
- 2 tablespoons soy sauce
- 1 tablespoon honey
- 1 tablespoon sesame oil
- 1 tablespoon rice vinegar
- 1 tablespoon fresh ginger, grated
- 2 cloves garlic, minced
- 1 teaspoon Chinese five-spice powder
- Salt and black pepper, to taste

For Skewering:

- Bamboo or metal skewers, soaked if using bamboo
- Sliced green onions, for garnish
- Sesame seeds, for garnish
- Lime wedges, for serving

Instructions:

In a bowl, whisk together all the marinade ingredients: hoisin sauce, soy sauce, honey, sesame oil, rice vinegar, grated ginger, minced garlic, Chinese five-spice powder, salt, and black pepper.

Place the pork cubes in a large bowl or a resealable plastic bag.

Pour the marinade over the pork, ensuring all pieces are well coated. Marinate in the refrigerator for at least 2 hours, or ideally overnight, to allow the flavors to infuse.

Preheat your grill or grill pan to medium-high heat.

Thread the marinated pork cubes onto the skewers.

Grill the pork skewers for about 8-10 minutes, turning occasionally, until they are cooked through and have a nice char on the edges.

Garnish the Hoisin and Ginger Pork Skewers with sliced green onions and sesame seeds.

Serve the skewers with lime wedges on the side for squeezing.

Optionally, you can brush additional hoisin sauce on the skewers during the last few minutes of grilling for extra flavor.

These Hoisin and Ginger Pork Skewers are a delicious blend of sweet, savory, and aromatic flavors. The marinade infuses the pork with a rich taste, and grilling adds a smoky char that enhances the overall experience. Serve these skewers as a delightful appetizer or as part of a main course, and enjoy the enticing combination of hoisin and ginger in every bite!

Southern BBQ Pulled Pork Sandwiches

Ingredients:

For the Pulled Pork:

- 4-5 pounds pork shoulder or pork butt
- 2 tablespoons brown sugar
- 1 tablespoon paprika
- 1 tablespoon garlic powder
- 1 tablespoon onion powder
- 1 tablespoon chili powder
- 1 tablespoon cumin
- 1 tablespoon mustard powder
- 1 tablespoon salt
- 1 teaspoon black pepper
- 1 cup apple cider vinegar
- 1 cup chicken broth or water
- 1 cup barbecue sauce (plus extra for serving)
- Sandwich buns

For the Coleslaw:

- 4 cups shredded cabbage (green and purple mix)
- 1 carrot, grated
- 1/2 cup mayonnaise
- 2 tablespoons apple cider vinegar
- 1 tablespoon honey
- Salt and black pepper, to taste

Instructions:

For the Pulled Pork:

In a small bowl, mix together brown sugar, paprika, garlic powder, onion powder, chili powder, cumin, mustard powder, salt, and black pepper to create a dry rub. Rub the dry rub all over the pork shoulder, ensuring it's well coated. Let it sit for at least 30 minutes or refrigerate overnight for better flavor penetration.
Preheat your smoker or grill to 225°F (107°C).

Place the seasoned pork shoulder on the smoker or grill and cook indirectly for about 5-6 hours or until the internal temperature reaches 200°F (93°C).
While the pork is smoking, mix together apple cider vinegar, chicken broth or water, and barbecue sauce in a bowl.
After the pork reaches the desired temperature, remove it from the smoker or grill and let it rest for about 30 minutes.
Shred the pork using two forks or your hands. Remove any excess fat.
Mix the shredded pork with the barbecue sauce mixture, ensuring it's well coated.

For the Coleslaw:

In a large bowl, combine shredded cabbage and grated carrot.
In a separate bowl, whisk together mayonnaise, apple cider vinegar, honey, salt, and black pepper.
Pour the dressing over the cabbage mixture and toss until well combined.

Assembling the Sandwiches:

Toast the sandwich buns on the grill or in the oven.
Spoon a generous portion of the pulled pork onto the bottom half of each bun.
Top the pulled pork with a scoop of coleslaw.
Place the top half of the bun on the coleslaw to complete the sandwich.
Serve the Southern BBQ Pulled Pork Sandwiches with extra barbecue sauce on the side.

These Southern BBQ Pulled Pork Sandwiches are a classic comfort food favorite. The slow-smoked, seasoned pork shoulder is tender and flavorful, and the addition of coleslaw adds a refreshing crunch. Enjoy these sandwiches for a delicious and satisfying meal, perfect for gatherings or a casual weekend barbecue!

Lemon Garlic Butter Pork Chops

Ingredients:

- 4 bone-in pork chops
- Salt and black pepper, to taste
- 2 tablespoons olive oil
- 4 cloves garlic, minced
- Zest of 1 lemon
- Juice of 1 lemon
- 1/2 cup chicken broth
- 1/4 cup white wine (optional)
- 2 tablespoons unsalted butter
- 2 tablespoons fresh parsley, chopped (for garnish)

Instructions:

Season the pork chops with salt and black pepper on both sides.
In a large skillet, heat olive oil over medium-high heat.
Add the pork chops to the skillet and sear for 3-4 minutes per side, or until golden brown. Ensure they reach an internal temperature of 145°F (63°C).
Remove the pork chops from the skillet and set them aside.
In the same skillet, add minced garlic and sauté for about 1 minute until fragrant.
Deglaze the skillet with white wine (if using), scraping up any browned bits from the bottom.
Add chicken broth, lemon zest, and lemon juice to the skillet. Bring the mixture to a simmer.
Reduce the heat to low and stir in the unsalted butter until melted and the sauce thickens slightly.
Return the seared pork chops to the skillet, spooning the lemon garlic butter sauce over them.
Continue cooking for an additional 2-3 minutes, allowing the pork chops to soak up the flavors of the sauce.
Garnish the Lemon Garlic Butter Pork Chops with chopped fresh parsley.
Serve the pork chops with the lemon garlic butter sauce drizzled over the top.

These Lemon Garlic Butter Pork Chops are a quick and flavorful dish that combines the zesty brightness of lemon with the rich taste of garlic and butter. The result is a delicious and juicy pork chop that is perfect for a weeknight dinner or a special occasion. Enjoy the delightful balance of citrusy and savory flavors in every bite!

Cuban Sandwich with Mojo-Marinated Pork

Ingredients:

For the Mojo-Marinated Pork:

- 2 pounds pork shoulder or pork loin, thinly sliced
- 1 cup orange juice
- 1/2 cup lime juice
- 1/4 cup olive oil
- 6 cloves garlic, minced
- 1 teaspoon cumin
- 1 teaspoon oregano
- Salt and black pepper, to taste

For the Cuban Sandwich:

- Cuban bread or French bread, sliced lengthwise
- Mojo-marinated pork slices
- Swiss cheese slices
- Smoked ham slices
- Dill pickles, sliced
- Yellow mustard
- Butter, for grilling

Instructions:

For the Mojo-Marinated Pork:

In a bowl, whisk together orange juice, lime juice, olive oil, minced garlic, cumin, oregano, salt, and black pepper to create the marinade.
Place the thinly sliced pork in a resealable plastic bag or a shallow dish.
Pour the mojo marinade over the pork, ensuring it's well-coated. Marinate in the refrigerator for at least 4 hours or overnight for maximum flavor.
Preheat your grill or grill pan to medium-high heat.
Remove the pork from the marinade, allowing any excess to drip off.
Grill the marinated pork slices for about 3-4 minutes per side or until fully cooked and slightly charred.

For the Cuban Sandwich:

Preheat a panini press or a large skillet over medium heat.
Assemble the Cuban sandwich by layering Swiss cheese slices, mojo-marinated pork slices, smoked ham slices, and dill pickle slices on the sliced bread.
Spread yellow mustard on the other half of the bread.
Close the sandwich, and spread butter on the outer sides of the bread.
Place the sandwich on the panini press or in the skillet.
Grill the Cuban sandwich for about 3-4 minutes on each side, or until the bread is toasted, the cheese is melted, and the fillings are heated through.
Remove the sandwich from the press or skillet and let it rest for a minute.
Slice the Cuban Sandwich diagonally and serve.

This Cuban Sandwich with Mojo-Marinated Pork captures the essence of Cuban cuisine with its vibrant flavors and layers of deliciousness. The mojo-marinated pork adds a zesty and aromatic touch, complemented by the classic combination of Swiss cheese, smoked ham, pickles, and mustard. Grilled to perfection, this Cuban sandwich is a delightful treat for lunch or dinner. Enjoy the fusion of flavors in each satisfying bite!

Pineapple Teriyaki Pork Burgers

Ingredients:

For the Pork Patties:

- 1.5 pounds ground pork
- 1/2 cup breadcrumbs
- 1/4 cup green onions, finely chopped
- 2 cloves garlic, minced
- 1 tablespoon soy sauce
- 1 teaspoon sesame oil
- 1/2 teaspoon ground ginger
- Salt and black pepper, to taste

For the Pineapple Teriyaki Glaze:

- 1 cup pineapple juice
- 1/4 cup soy sauce
- 2 tablespoons brown sugar
- 1 tablespoon rice vinegar
- 1 teaspoon sesame oil
- 1 teaspoon cornstarch (optional, for thickening)

For Assembling the Burgers:

- Burger buns
- Pineapple rings, grilled
- Lettuce leaves
- Red onion, thinly sliced
- Swiss or provolone cheese slices
- Teriyaki mayonnaise (optional)

Instructions:

For the Pork Patties:

In a large bowl, combine ground pork, breadcrumbs, green onions, minced garlic, soy sauce, sesame oil, ground ginger, salt, and black pepper.
Mix the ingredients until well combined, but avoid overmixing to keep the patties tender.

Divide the mixture into equal portions and shape them into burger patties.
Preheat your grill or grill pan over medium-high heat.
Grill the pork patties for about 5-6 minutes per side, or until fully cooked and nicely charred.

For the Pineapple Teriyaki Glaze:

In a saucepan, combine pineapple juice, soy sauce, brown sugar, rice vinegar, and sesame oil.
Bring the mixture to a simmer over medium heat.
Optional: If you prefer a thicker glaze, mix a teaspoon of cornstarch with a little water to create a slurry. Stir it into the simmering sauce and continue cooking until thickened.
Remove the glaze from heat and set it aside.

For Assembling the Burgers:

Toast the burger buns on the grill or in the oven.
Brush the grilled pork patties with the Pineapple Teriyaki Glaze.
Assemble the burgers by placing a grilled pork patty on the bottom half of each bun.
Top each patty with a grilled pineapple ring, lettuce leaves, red onion slices, and Swiss or provolone cheese.
Optionally, spread teriyaki mayonnaise on the top half of the bun.
Place the top bun on the assembled ingredients to complete the burger.
Serve the Pineapple Teriyaki Pork Burgers with additional glaze on the side for dipping.

These Pineapple Teriyaki Pork Burgers bring a burst of tropical flavors to the classic burger experience. The juicy and flavorful pork patties, combined with the sweet and savory pineapple teriyaki glaze, create a mouthwatering delight. Grilled pineapple rings and a variety of toppings make these burgers a perfect choice for a summery and satisfying meal. Enjoy the delicious fusion of teriyaki and pineapple in every bite!

Five-Spice Roast Pork Belly

Ingredients:

- 2 pounds pork belly, skin-on
- 2 tablespoons Chinese five-spice powder
- 1 tablespoon salt
- 1 tablespoon sugar
- 1 teaspoon white pepper
- 2 tablespoons soy sauce
- 2 tablespoons Shaoxing wine (Chinese rice wine) or dry sherry
- 2 tablespoons honey
- 2 cloves garlic, minced
- 1 tablespoon ginger, grated
- 1 tablespoon vegetable oil

Instructions:

Preheat your oven to 375°F (190°C).
Score the pork belly skin with a sharp knife in a crosshatch pattern, being careful not to cut too deeply into the meat.
In a bowl, mix together the Chinese five-spice powder, salt, sugar, and white pepper.
Rub the spice mixture all over the pork belly, ensuring it's well-coated on all sides.
In a separate bowl, combine soy sauce, Shaoxing wine, honey, minced garlic, and grated ginger to create the marinade.
Place the pork belly in a large dish or resealable plastic bag and pour the marinade over it. Massage the marinade into the meat, ensuring it gets into the scored skin.
Marinate the pork belly in the refrigerator for at least 4 hours, or preferably overnight.
Remove the pork belly from the refrigerator and let it come to room temperature for about 30 minutes.
Heat vegetable oil in an oven-safe skillet or roasting pan over medium-high heat.
Sear the pork belly, skin-side down, until the skin is golden and crispy, about 5-7 minutes.
Flip the pork belly, skin-side up, and pour any remaining marinade over the top.
Transfer the skillet or roasting pan to the preheated oven and roast for about 1.5 to 2 hours, or until the pork is tender and the skin is crispy.
Optional: Place the pork belly under the broiler for a few minutes to further crisp the skin.

Once cooked, remove the pork belly from the oven and let it rest for 10-15 minutes before slicing.
Slice the Five-Spice Roast Pork Belly into pieces and serve.

This Five-Spice Roast Pork Belly recipe showcases the aromatic and rich flavors of Chinese five-spice powder, creating a deliciously crispy and flavorful dish. The combination of spices, soy sauce, and honey results in a perfect balance of sweet, savory, and aromatic notes. Enjoy this roast pork belly as a main course or add it to your favorite Asian-inspired dishes!

Pomegranate Glazed Pork Tenderloin

Ingredients:

For the Pork Tenderloin:

- 2 pork tenderloins (about 1 to 1.5 pounds each)
- Salt and black pepper, to taste
- 2 tablespoons olive oil

For the Pomegranate Glaze:

- 1 cup pomegranate juice
- 1/4 cup balsamic vinegar
- 1/4 cup honey
- 2 tablespoons soy sauce
- 2 cloves garlic, minced
- 1 teaspoon Dijon mustard
- 1 teaspoon cornstarch (optional, for thickening)

Instructions:

Preheat your oven to 375°F (190°C).
Season the pork tenderloins with salt and black pepper on all sides.
In an oven-safe skillet, heat olive oil over medium-high heat.
Sear the pork tenderloins on all sides until browned, about 2-3 minutes per side.
While the pork is searing, prepare the pomegranate glaze. In a small saucepan, combine pomegranate juice, balsamic vinegar, honey, soy sauce, minced garlic, and Dijon mustard.
Bring the mixture to a simmer over medium heat. If you prefer a thicker glaze, mix cornstarch with a little water to create a slurry and stir it into the sauce. Simmer until the glaze thickens.
Pour the pomegranate glaze over the seared pork tenderloins.
Transfer the skillet to the preheated oven and roast for about 15-20 minutes, or until the internal temperature of the pork reaches 145°F (63°C).
Baste the pork with the glaze every 5-7 minutes during the roasting process.
Optional: For a caramelized finish, you can broil the pork for a few minutes after roasting.
Once cooked, remove the skillet from the oven and let the pork tenderloins rest for 5-10 minutes.
Slice the Pomegranate Glazed Pork Tenderloin into rounds and serve with any remaining glaze.

This Pomegranate Glazed Pork Tenderloin recipe offers a perfect balance of sweet and tangy flavors. The pomegranate glaze adds a delightful touch of richness to the tender and succulent pork tenderloin. Serve it as an elegant main course for a special occasion or a festive dinner. Enjoy the burst of flavors in every bite!

German Sauerkraut and Pork

Ingredients:

- 1.5 to 2 pounds pork shoulder or pork chops

- Salt and black pepper, to taste
- 2 tablespoons vegetable oil
- 1 large onion, thinly sliced
- 2 cloves garlic, minced
- 1 pound sauerkraut, drained and rinsed
- 1 tablespoon caraway seeds
- 1 cup chicken or beef broth
- 2 bay leaves
- 1 tablespoon Dijon mustard
- 2 apples, peeled, cored, and sliced (optional)
- 1/2 cup dry white wine (optional)
- Chopped fresh parsley, for garnish

Instructions:

Preheat your oven to 325°F (163°C).
Season the pork with salt and black pepper on all sides.
In a large oven-safe Dutch oven or skillet, heat vegetable oil over medium-high heat.
Sear the pork on all sides until browned, about 2-3 minutes per side. Remove the pork from the pot and set it aside.
In the same pot, add sliced onions and sauté until softened, about 5 minutes.
Add minced garlic and sauté for an additional 1-2 minutes until fragrant.
Stir in sauerkraut and caraway seeds, cooking for 2-3 minutes.
Pour in chicken or beef broth, Dijon mustard, and add bay leaves.
Return the seared pork to the pot, nestling it into the sauerkraut mixture.
If using, add sliced apples and pour dry white wine over the top.
Bring the mixture to a simmer.
Cover the pot with a lid and transfer it to the preheated oven.
Bake for about 2 to 2.5 hours, or until the pork is tender and fully cooked.
Optional: For a crispy finish, remove the lid during the last 20-30 minutes of cooking.
Once cooked, discard the bay leaves and garnish with chopped fresh parsley.
Serve the German Sauerkraut and Pork over mashed potatoes, boiled potatoes, or with crusty bread.

This German Sauerkraut and Pork recipe combines the savory richness of pork with the tangy and flavorful sauerkraut, creating a comforting and hearty dish. The addition of caraway seeds, mustard, and optional apples enhances the traditional German flavors. Serve this delightful dish for a satisfying meal that captures the essence of German cuisine. Enjoy the delicious blend of savory and tangy notes in each forkful!

Miso-Glazed Pork Belly

Ingredients:

For the Pork Belly:

- 2 pounds pork belly, skin-on
- Salt and black pepper, to taste

For the Miso Glaze:

- 1/4 cup white or red miso paste
- 2 tablespoons sake
- 2 tablespoons mirin
- 2 tablespoons soy sauce
- 2 tablespoons brown sugar
- 1 tablespoon grated fresh ginger
- 2 cloves garlic, minced

Instructions:

Preheat your oven to 375°F (190°C).
Score the skin of the pork belly with a sharp knife in a crosshatch pattern, being careful not to cut too deeply into the meat.
Season the pork belly with salt and black pepper on all sides, including the skin.
Place the pork belly in an oven-safe dish or roasting pan, skin-side up.
In a bowl, whisk together the miso paste, sake, mirin, soy sauce, brown sugar, grated ginger, and minced garlic to create the miso glaze.
Brush or rub the miso glaze all over the pork belly, ensuring it gets into the scored skin.
Roast the pork belly in the preheated oven for about 1.5 to 2 hours, or until the pork is cooked through and the skin is crispy.
Optional: If the skin needs additional crisping, you can place the pork belly under the broiler for a few minutes, keeping a close eye to prevent burning.
Once cooked, remove the pork belly from the oven and let it rest for 10-15 minutes before slicing.
Slice the Miso-Glazed Pork Belly into pieces and serve.

This Miso-Glazed Pork Belly recipe offers a delightful combination of sweet, savory, and umami flavors. The miso glaze provides a rich and flavorful coating to the pork belly, while the roasting process results in tender meat and crispy skin. Serve this dish as a main course with your favorite side dishes, and enjoy the unique and delicious taste of miso-glazed pork belly!

Bacon-Wrapped Pork Medallions

Ingredients:

- 1.5 to 2 pounds pork tenderloin, trimmed and cut into 1-inch thick medallions

- Salt and black pepper, to taste
- 1 teaspoon garlic powder
- 1 teaspoon onion powder
- 1 teaspoon smoked paprika
- 1 tablespoon olive oil
- 8-10 slices bacon
- 2 tablespoons maple syrup (optional, for brushing)

Instructions:

Preheat your oven to 375°F (190°C).
Season the pork medallions with salt, black pepper, garlic powder, onion powder, and smoked paprika.
In a large skillet, heat olive oil over medium-high heat.
Sear the pork medallions for about 1-2 minutes on each side until browned.
Remove from the skillet and set aside.
Wrap each pork medallion with a slice of bacon, securing it with toothpicks if needed.
Place the bacon-wrapped pork medallions on a baking sheet lined with parchment paper.
Optional: Brush the bacon-wrapped pork with maple syrup for a touch of sweetness.
Bake in the preheated oven for 20-25 minutes or until the bacon is crispy and the pork reaches an internal temperature of 145°F (63°C).
If you prefer a crispier bacon exterior, you can broil the medallions for a few minutes, keeping a close eye to prevent burning.
Once cooked, remove the bacon-wrapped pork medallions from the oven and let them rest for a few minutes.
Remove toothpicks before serving.
Serve the Bacon-Wrapped Pork Medallions as a delicious and savory appetizer or as a main course with your favorite sides.

These Bacon-Wrapped Pork Medallions are a mouthwatering combination of juicy pork and crispy bacon, making them a perfect option for a flavorful appetizer or a delicious main course. The seasoning and optional maple syrup add extra depth to the taste, creating a dish that's sure to satisfy your cravings for savory and smoky flavors. Enjoy these succulent bacon-wrapped delights for a delightful meal!

Moroccan Spiced Pork Tagine

Ingredients:

- 2 pounds pork shoulder or pork loin, cut into cubes

- 2 tablespoons olive oil
- 1 large onion, finely chopped
- 3 cloves garlic, minced
- 1 teaspoon ground cumin
- 1 teaspoon ground coriander
- 1 teaspoon ground cinnamon
- 1 teaspoon ground ginger
- 1 teaspoon paprika
- 1/2 teaspoon cayenne pepper (adjust to taste)
- Salt and black pepper, to taste
- 1 can (14 ounces) diced tomatoes, undrained
- 1 cup chicken broth
- 1 cup dried apricots, halved
- 1/2 cup green olives, pitted and halved
- 1/4 cup chopped fresh cilantro or parsley, for garnish
- Cooked couscous or rice, for serving

Instructions:

In a large, heavy-bottomed pot or tagine, heat olive oil over medium-high heat.
Add the chopped onion and sauté until softened, about 5 minutes.
Add minced garlic and sauté for an additional 1-2 minutes until fragrant.
Add the pork cubes to the pot and brown on all sides.
Stir in ground cumin, ground coriander, ground cinnamon, ground ginger, paprika, cayenne pepper, salt, and black pepper. Cook for 1-2 minutes until the spices are fragrant.
Pour in diced tomatoes with their juices and chicken broth. Bring the mixture to a simmer.
Reduce the heat to low, cover the pot, and let it simmer for about 1.5 to 2 hours, or until the pork is tender.
Add dried apricots and green olives to the pot, stirring to combine.
Continue simmering for an additional 15-20 minutes until the apricots are softened and the flavors meld together.
Adjust seasoning if needed and remove from heat.
Serve the Moroccan Spiced Pork Tagine over cooked couscous or rice.
Garnish with chopped fresh cilantro or parsley before serving.

This Moroccan Spiced Pork Tagine is a flavorful and aromatic dish that brings together the exotic spices of Moroccan cuisine with tender pork, dried apricots, and green olives.

The slow simmering process allows the flavors to meld together, creating a deliciously rich and satisfying stew. Serve it over couscous or rice for a complete and hearty meal. Enjoy the unique taste of Morocco in every bite!

Caramelized Onion and Apple Stuffed Pork Chops

Ingredients:

For the Stuffed Pork Chops:

- 4 bone-in pork chops
- Salt and black pepper, to taste
- 2 tablespoons olive oil

For the Caramelized Onion and Apple Filling:

- 2 large onions, thinly sliced
- 2 apples, peeled, cored, and diced (such as Granny Smith or Honeycrisp)
- 2 tablespoons unsalted butter
- 1 tablespoon brown sugar
- 1 teaspoon balsamic vinegar
- 1 teaspoon fresh thyme leaves (or 1/2 teaspoon dried thyme)
- Salt and black pepper, to taste

Instructions:

Preheat your oven to 375°F (190°C).
Season the pork chops with salt and black pepper on both sides.
In a large oven-safe skillet, heat olive oil over medium-high heat.
Sear the pork chops on both sides until browned, about 2-3 minutes per side.
Remove the chops from the skillet and set them aside.
In the same skillet, add unsalted butter and sliced onions. Cook the onions over medium heat, stirring occasionally, until they become caramelized and golden brown, about 15-20 minutes.
Add diced apples to the caramelized onions and continue cooking for an additional 5 minutes.
Stir in brown sugar, balsamic vinegar, fresh thyme, salt, and black pepper. Cook for another 2-3 minutes until the apples are softened.
Create a pocket in each pork chop by slicing horizontally into the side of the chop, being careful not to cut all the way through.
Stuff each pork chop with the caramelized onion and apple filling.
Place the stuffed pork chops back into the skillet.
Transfer the skillet to the preheated oven and roast for about 20-25 minutes, or until the internal temperature of the pork reaches 145°F (63°C).
Optional: For a caramelized finish, you can broil the pork chops for a few minutes after roasting.

Remove the skillet from the oven and let the stuffed pork chops rest for 5 minutes before serving.

Serve the Caramelized Onion and Apple Stuffed Pork Chops with any remaining filling spooned over the top.

These Caramelized Onion and Apple Stuffed Pork Chops offer a delightful combination of savory and sweet flavors. The caramelized onion and apple filling adds a burst of sweetness and complexity to the tender and succulent pork chops. Serve them for a special dinner occasion or whenever you want to impress with a delicious and elegant dish. Enjoy the rich and comforting taste in every bite!

Tex-Mex Pork Carnitas

Ingredients:

For the Pork:

- 3-4 pounds pork shoulder, cut into chunks
- 1 tablespoon vegetable oil
- Salt and black pepper, to taste
- 1 teaspoon ground cumin
- 1 teaspoon chili powder
- 1 teaspoon paprika
- 1 teaspoon garlic powder
- 1 teaspoon onion powder
- 1/2 teaspoon cayenne pepper (optional, for extra heat)
- 1 cup orange juice
- 1/4 cup lime juice
- 1 onion, sliced
- 4 cloves garlic, minced
- 1 bay leaf

For Serving:

- Corn or flour tortillas
- Salsa
- Guacamole
- Shredded lettuce
- Chopped tomatoes
- Fresh cilantro
- Lime wedges

Instructions:

Preheat your oven to 325°F (163°C).
In a large oven-safe pot or Dutch oven, heat vegetable oil over medium-high heat.
Season the pork chunks with salt, black pepper, ground cumin, chili powder, paprika, garlic powder, onion powder, and cayenne pepper.
Sear the pork in the hot oil until browned on all sides.
Pour in orange juice and lime juice, scraping up any browned bits from the bottom of the pot.
Add sliced onions, minced garlic, and bay leaf to the pot.
Cover the pot with a lid and transfer it to the preheated oven.
Braise the pork in the oven for 2.5 to 3 hours, or until the meat is tender and easily shreds with a fork.
Once the pork is cooked, remove it from the oven and shred it using two forks.

Optional: For crispy carnitas, transfer the shredded pork to a baking sheet and broil for a few minutes until the edges are golden and crispy.

Serve the Tex-Mex Pork Carnitas in tortillas with your favorite toppings such as salsa, guacamole, shredded lettuce, chopped tomatoes, fresh cilantro, and lime wedges.

Enjoy the Tex-Mex Pork Carnitas as tacos, burritos, or in any other way you prefer!

These Tex-Mex Pork Carnitas are flavorful and tender, with a perfect balance of spices and citrusy notes. Serve them in tortillas with your favorite toppings for a delicious and satisfying meal. Whether you're hosting a gathering or having a casual dinner, these carnitas are sure to be a hit with their bold and authentic Tex-Mex flavors!

Fig and Port Wine Glazed Ham

Ingredients:

- 1 bone-in ham (about 8-10 pounds)
- 1 cup port wine

- 1 cup fig preserves
- 1/2 cup Dijon mustard
- 1/4 cup brown sugar
- 2 tablespoons balsamic vinegar
- 1 teaspoon ground cinnamon
- 1/2 teaspoon ground cloves
- 1/4 teaspoon ground nutmeg
- Salt and black pepper, to taste
- Fresh figs, for garnish (optional)

Instructions:

Preheat your oven to 325°F (163°C).

Place the ham in a roasting pan, and score the surface in a diamond pattern with a sharp knife.

In a saucepan over medium heat, combine port wine, fig preserves, Dijon mustard, brown sugar, balsamic vinegar, ground cinnamon, ground cloves, ground nutmeg, salt, and black pepper.

Stir the mixture well and bring it to a simmer. Let it simmer for about 5-7 minutes, allowing the flavors to meld and the glaze to thicken slightly.

Brush a generous amount of the fig and port wine glaze over the surface of the ham, making sure to get it into the scored areas.

Roast the ham in the preheated oven, basting with the glaze every 20-30 minutes, until the internal temperature reaches 140°F (60°C). This typically takes about 15-18 minutes per pound.

Optional: For a caramelized finish, you can broil the ham for the last few minutes, watching carefully to prevent burning.

Once the ham is cooked, remove it from the oven and let it rest for about 15-20 minutes before carving.

Transfer the remaining glaze to a saucepan and heat it on the stove until warmed through.

Carve the Fig and Port Wine Glazed Ham and serve it with the warmed glaze on the side.

Optionally, garnish with fresh figs for a decorative touch.

This Fig and Port Wine Glazed Ham combines the rich and savory flavors of ham with the sweet and fruity notes of fig and port wine. The glaze adds a beautiful caramelized finish, making it an elegant and flavorful centerpiece for holiday gatherings or special occasions. Enjoy the succulent and tender ham with a touch of sophistication in every bite!

Thai Coconut Curry Pork

Ingredients:

- 1.5 pounds pork tenderloin or pork loin, thinly sliced
- 2 tablespoons vegetable oil

- 1 onion, thinly sliced
- 3 cloves garlic, minced
- 1 red bell pepper, thinly sliced
- 1 yellow bell pepper, thinly sliced
- 2 tablespoons red curry paste
- 1 can (14 ounces) coconut milk
- 1 tablespoon fish sauce
- 1 tablespoon soy sauce
- 1 tablespoon brown sugar
- 1 tablespoon lime juice
- 1 teaspoon grated fresh ginger
- Fresh cilantro leaves, for garnish
- Cooked jasmine rice, for serving

Instructions:

In a large skillet or wok, heat vegetable oil over medium-high heat.
Add thinly sliced pork and cook until browned on all sides. Remove the pork from the skillet and set it aside.
In the same skillet, add sliced onion and cook until softened.
Add minced garlic and cook for an additional 1-2 minutes until fragrant.
Stir in red curry paste and cook for another 1-2 minutes, allowing the flavors to meld.
Add thinly sliced red and yellow bell peppers to the skillet and cook until they begin to soften.
Pour in coconut milk, fish sauce, soy sauce, brown sugar, and lime juice. Stir well to combine.
Return the cooked pork to the skillet, along with any juices it released. Add grated fresh ginger.
Simmer the Thai Coconut Curry Pork for 10-15 minutes, allowing the flavors to infuse and the pork to fully cook.
Adjust the seasoning to taste, adding more fish sauce, soy sauce, or lime juice if needed.
Serve the Thai Coconut Curry Pork over cooked jasmine rice.
Garnish with fresh cilantro leaves before serving.

This Thai Coconut Curry Pork is a delicious and aromatic dish that combines tender slices of pork with the rich and flavorful Thai coconut curry sauce. The blend of red curry paste, coconut milk, and a balance of savory, sweet, and tangy ingredients creates a delightful experience for your taste buds. Serve it over jasmine rice for a satisfying and comforting meal with a Thai-inspired twist!

Bourbon and Brown Sugar Pork Ribs

Ingredients:

For the Pork Ribs:

- 2 racks of baby back pork ribs
- Salt and black pepper, to taste

For the Bourbon and Brown Sugar Glaze:

- 1 cup bourbon
- 1 cup brown sugar
- 1/2 cup ketchup
- 1/4 cup soy sauce
- 2 tablespoons Dijon mustard
- 2 tablespoons Worcestershire sauce
- 2 cloves garlic, minced
- 1 teaspoon smoked paprika
- 1/2 teaspoon cayenne pepper (optional, for heat)

Instructions:

Preheat your oven to 275°F (135°C).
Remove the membrane from the back of the ribs and season them with salt and black pepper.
Place the ribs on a baking sheet or in a roasting pan, bone side down.
Cover the ribs tightly with aluminum foil.
Bake the ribs in the preheated oven for 2.5 to 3 hours, or until they are tender and cooked through.
While the ribs are baking, prepare the Bourbon and Brown Sugar Glaze. In a saucepan over medium heat, combine bourbon, brown sugar, ketchup, soy sauce, Dijon mustard, Worcestershire sauce, minced garlic, smoked paprika, and cayenne pepper. Bring the mixture to a simmer and cook for 15-20 minutes, or until the glaze thickens.
Preheat your grill or broiler.
Remove the ribs from the oven and baste them generously with the Bourbon and Brown Sugar Glaze.
Grill or broil the ribs for 5-10 minutes, basting with the glaze and turning occasionally, until the ribs are caramelized and have a slightly charred appearance.
Let the Bourbon and Brown Sugar Pork Ribs rest for a few minutes before slicing.
Serve the ribs with additional glaze on the side.
Enjoy the Bourbon and Brown Sugar Pork Ribs with your favorite side dishes!

These Bourbon and Brown Sugar Pork Ribs are a delightful combination of sweet, savory, and smoky flavors. The slow oven-baking ensures tender and juicy ribs, while the bourbon and brown sugar glaze adds a rich and caramelized finish. Whether you're hosting a barbecue or enjoying a special dinner, these ribs are sure to be a crowd-pleaser. Serve them with your favorite sides for a finger-licking good meal!

Pesto-Stuffed Grilled Pork Chops

Ingredients:

For the Pesto:

- 2 cups fresh basil leaves, packed
- 1/2 cup grated Parmesan cheese
- 1/2 cup pine nuts or walnuts
- 3 cloves garlic, peeled
- 1/2 cup extra-virgin olive oil
- Salt and black pepper, to taste

For the Grilled Pork Chops:

- 4 bone-in pork chops
- Salt and black pepper, to taste
- Olive oil, for brushing

Instructions:

For the Pesto:

In a food processor, combine fresh basil, grated Parmesan cheese, pine nuts or walnuts, and garlic.
Pulse until the ingredients are finely chopped.
With the food processor running, slowly drizzle in the extra-virgin olive oil until the pesto reaches a smooth consistency.
Season the pesto with salt and black pepper to taste. Set aside.

For the Grilled Pork Chops:

Preheat your grill to medium-high heat.
Season the bone-in pork chops with salt and black pepper on both sides.
Using a sharp knife, make a horizontal slit in each pork chop to create a pocket for the pesto stuffing.
Stuff each pork chop with a generous spoonful of the prepared pesto.
Secure the openings with toothpicks if needed.
Brush the stuffed pork chops with olive oil to prevent sticking on the grill.
Place the pork chops on the preheated grill and cook for about 5-7 minutes per side, or until they reach your desired level of doneness.
Optional: During the last few minutes of grilling, baste the pork chops with additional pesto for extra flavor.

Remove the Pesto-Stuffed Grilled Pork Chops from the grill and let them rest for a few minutes.
Serve the pork chops with any remaining pesto drizzled on top.

These Pesto-Stuffed Grilled Pork Chops are a delicious and flavorful option for your barbecue or grilled dinner. The pesto stuffing adds a burst of fresh and herby taste, complementing the juicy pork chops. Enjoy these grilled delights with your favorite sides for a perfect outdoor meal.

Vietnamese Lemongrass Pork Banh Mi

Ingredients:

For the Lemongrass Marinade:

- 1.5 pounds pork shoulder or pork loin, thinly sliced
- 3 stalks lemongrass, finely chopped
- 4 cloves garlic, minced
- 2 shallots, minced
- 2 tablespoons fish sauce
- 2 tablespoons soy sauce
- 2 tablespoons vegetable oil
- 1 tablespoon honey or brown sugar
- 1 teaspoon ground black pepper

For the Banh Mi:

- Baguettes or French bread
- Mayonnaise
- Sriracha sauce (optional)
- Pickled daikon and carrots (recipe below)
- Fresh cilantro leaves
- Sliced cucumber
- Jalapeño slices (optional)

For the Pickled Daikon and Carrots:

- 1 cup julienned daikon radish
- 1 cup julienned carrots
- 1/2 cup rice vinegar
- 1/4 cup water
- 2 tablespoons sugar
- 1 teaspoon salt

Instructions:

For the Lemongrass Marinade:

In a bowl, combine chopped lemongrass, minced garlic, minced shallots, fish sauce, soy sauce, vegetable oil, honey or brown sugar, and ground black pepper. Add the thinly sliced pork to the marinade, ensuring it's well-coated.

Cover the bowl and let the pork marinate in the refrigerator for at least 2 hours or overnight for maximum flavor.

For the Pickled Daikon and Carrots:

In a bowl, mix rice vinegar, water, sugar, and salt until the sugar and salt dissolve.
Add julienned daikon and carrots to the vinegar mixture, ensuring they are submerged.
Let the daikon and carrots pickle in the refrigerator for at least 1 hour.

For Assembling the Banh Mi:

Preheat your grill or grill pan to medium-high heat.
Grill the marinated pork slices for about 2-3 minutes per side or until fully cooked and slightly charred.
Slice the baguettes or French bread lengthwise.
Spread mayonnaise on one side of the bread and Sriracha sauce, if desired, on the other side.
Arrange the grilled lemongrass pork on the bread.
Top with pickled daikon and carrots, fresh cilantro leaves, sliced cucumber, and jalapeño slices, if using.
Close the sandwich and press it together gently.
Serve the Vietnamese Lemongrass Pork Banh Mi immediately and enjoy!

This Vietnamese Lemongrass Pork Banh Mi is a delightful sandwich that combines the aromatic flavors of lemongrass-marinated pork with the freshness of pickled vegetables and the creaminess of mayonnaise. It's a perfect balance of savory, sweet, tangy, and spicy elements. Enjoy this iconic Vietnamese street food for a flavorful and satisfying meal!

Raspberry Balsamic Glazed Pork Tenderloin

Ingredients:

For the Pork Tenderloin:

- 2 pork tenderloins (about 1 to 1.5 pounds each)
- Salt and black pepper, to taste
- 2 tablespoons olive oil

For the Raspberry Balsamic Glaze:

- 1 cup fresh or frozen raspberries
- 1/2 cup balsamic vinegar
- 1/4 cup honey
- 2 tablespoons Dijon mustard
- 2 cloves garlic, minced
- 1 teaspoon soy sauce
- Salt and black pepper, to taste

Instructions:

Preheat your oven to 375°F (190°C).
Season the pork tenderloins with salt and black pepper on all sides.
In an oven-safe skillet, heat olive oil over medium-high heat.
Sear the pork tenderloins on all sides until browned, about 2-3 minutes per side.
While the pork is searing, prepare the Raspberry Balsamic Glaze. In a small saucepan, combine raspberries, balsamic vinegar, honey, Dijon mustard, minced garlic, soy sauce, salt, and black pepper.
Bring the mixture to a simmer over medium heat. Use a spoon to mash the raspberries and stir the ingredients together.
Simmer the glaze for about 5-7 minutes, or until it thickens slightly.
Pour the Raspberry Balsamic Glaze over the seared pork tenderloins in the skillet.
Transfer the skillet to the preheated oven and roast for about 15-20 minutes, or until the internal temperature of the pork reaches 145°F (63°C).
Baste the pork with the glaze every 5-7 minutes during the roasting process.
Optional: For a caramelized finish, you can broil the pork for a few minutes after roasting.
Once cooked, remove the skillet from the oven and let the pork tenderloins rest for 5-10 minutes.
Slice the Raspberry Balsamic Glazed Pork Tenderloin into rounds and serve with any remaining glaze.

This Raspberry Balsamic Glazed Pork Tenderloin recipe offers a perfect combination of sweet and tangy flavors, with the natural tartness of raspberries complementing the richness of balsamic vinegar. The glaze creates a glossy and flavorful coating for the succulent pork tenderloin. Serve this dish for a special occasion or a delightful weeknight dinner, and savor the deliciousness of this sweet and savory creation!

Garlic Parmesan Crusted Pork Chops

Ingredients:

For the Pork Chops:

- 4 bone-in pork chops
- Salt and black pepper, to taste

- 2 tablespoons olive oil

For the Garlic Parmesan Crust:

- 1 cup grated Parmesan cheese
- 1/2 cup breadcrumbs
- 4 cloves garlic, minced
- 2 teaspoons dried oregano
- 1 teaspoon dried thyme
- 1/2 teaspoon paprika
- 1/4 cup chopped fresh parsley
- 1/4 cup melted butter

Instructions:

Preheat your oven to 375°F (190°C).
Season the pork chops with salt and black pepper on both sides.
In a skillet, heat olive oil over medium-high heat.
Sear the pork chops on both sides until browned, about 2-3 minutes per side.
Remove the chops from the skillet and set them aside.
In a bowl, combine grated Parmesan cheese, breadcrumbs, minced garlic, dried oregano, dried thyme, paprika, chopped fresh parsley, and melted butter. Mix well to form the crust mixture.
Place the seared pork chops on a baking sheet lined with parchment paper or foil.
Press the Garlic Parmesan Crust mixture onto the top of each pork chop, ensuring an even coating.
Bake in the preheated oven for about 20-25 minutes or until the internal temperature of the pork reaches 145°F (63°C).
Optional: For a golden-brown crust, you can broil the pork chops for a few minutes after baking, keeping a close eye to prevent burning.
Once cooked, remove the Garlic Parmesan Crusted Pork Chops from the oven and let them rest for a few minutes before serving.
Serve the pork chops with your favorite side dishes.

These Garlic Parmesan Crusted Pork Chops are a delicious combination of savory, cheesy, and herby flavors. The crispy crust adds a delightful texture to the succulent pork chops. Serve them alongside roasted vegetables, mashed potatoes, or your preferred sides for a comforting and flavorful meal that's sure to be a hit at the dinner table!

Pineapple Jalapeño Pulled Pork Sliders

Ingredients:

For the Pulled Pork:

- 3-4 pounds pork shoulder or pork butt

- Salt and black pepper, to taste
- 1 tablespoon vegetable oil
- 1 onion, diced
- 3 cloves garlic, minced
- 1 cup pineapple juice
- 1 cup chicken broth
- 1 cup crushed pineapple (canned or fresh)
- 1/4 cup brown sugar
- 2 tablespoons soy sauce
- 2 teaspoons ground cumin
- 1 teaspoon smoked paprika
- 1 teaspoon chili powder
- 1 jalapeño, seeds removed and finely chopped

For the Sliders:

- Slider buns or small dinner rolls
- Coleslaw (optional, for topping)

Instructions:

For the Pulled Pork:

Preheat your oven to 325°F (163°C).
Season the pork shoulder or pork butt with salt and black pepper on all sides.
In a large oven-safe Dutch oven or skillet, heat vegetable oil over medium-high heat.
Sear the pork on all sides until browned. Remove the pork from the pot and set it aside.
In the same pot, add diced onion and sauté until softened.
Add minced garlic and sauté for an additional 1-2 minutes until fragrant.
Pour in pineapple juice, chicken broth, crushed pineapple, brown sugar, soy sauce, ground cumin, smoked paprika, chili powder, and chopped jalapeño. Stir well to combine.
Return the seared pork to the pot, nestling it into the pineapple mixture.
Bring the mixture to a simmer.
Cover the pot with a lid and transfer it to the preheated oven.

Bake for about 3 to 3.5 hours, or until the pork is tender and easily shreds with a fork.
Once cooked, remove the pork from the pot and shred it using two forks.
Optional: For a caramelized finish, you can place the shredded pork under the broiler for a few minutes, keeping a close eye to prevent burning.

For the Sliders:

Toast the slider buns or dinner rolls in the oven or on a skillet.
Fill each bun with a generous portion of the Pineapple Jalapeño Pulled Pork.
Optionally, top with coleslaw for added crunch and freshness.
Serve the Pineapple Jalapeño Pulled Pork Sliders and enjoy!

These Pineapple Jalapeño Pulled Pork Sliders offer a perfect balance of sweet, spicy, and savory flavors. The combination of pineapple, jalapeño, and a blend of spices creates a deliciously unique pulled pork. Serve them as sliders for a crowd-pleasing appetizer or main course. The addition of coleslaw adds a refreshing crunch to complement the tender and flavorful pulled pork. Enjoy these sliders at your next gathering or game day event!

Greek Gyro with Pork Souvlaki

Ingredients:

For the Pork Souvlaki:

- 1.5 pounds pork shoulder or pork loin, cut into chunks

- 1/4 cup olive oil
- 2 tablespoons red wine vinegar
- 3 cloves garlic, minced
- 1 teaspoon dried oregano
- 1 teaspoon dried thyme
- Salt and black pepper, to taste
- Wooden skewers, soaked in water

For the Tzatziki Sauce:

- 1 cup Greek yogurt
- 1 cucumber, peeled, seeded, and finely diced
- 2 cloves garlic, minced
- 1 tablespoon fresh dill, chopped
- 1 tablespoon fresh mint, chopped
- 1 tablespoon lemon juice
- Salt and black pepper, to taste

For Assembling the Gyro:

- Pita bread or flatbreads
- Sliced tomatoes
- Sliced red onions
- Fresh lettuce or shredded iceberg lettuce

Instructions:

For the Pork Souvlaki:

In a bowl, combine olive oil, red wine vinegar, minced garlic, dried oregano, dried thyme, salt, and black pepper.
Add the pork chunks to the marinade, ensuring they are well-coated.
Cover the bowl and let the pork marinate in the refrigerator for at least 1-2 hours, or overnight for maximum flavor.
Preheat your grill or grill pan to medium-high heat.
Thread the marinated pork chunks onto soaked wooden skewers.

Grill the pork skewers for about 10-15 minutes, turning occasionally, until the pork is fully cooked and has a nice char.

For the Tzatziki Sauce:

In a bowl, combine Greek yogurt, finely diced cucumber, minced garlic, chopped fresh dill, chopped fresh mint, lemon juice, salt, and black pepper.
Mix well to combine.
Refrigerate the Tzatziki sauce until ready to use.

For Assembling the Gyro:

Heat the pita bread or flatbreads according to package instructions.
Spread a generous amount of Tzatziki sauce on each piece of bread.
Place a few slices of grilled pork souvlaki on top of the Tzatziki.
Add sliced tomatoes, sliced red onions, and fresh lettuce or shredded iceberg lettuce.
Fold or roll the bread to form the gyro.
Serve the Greek Gyro with Pork Souvlaki and enjoy!

This Greek Gyro with Pork Souvlaki is a delicious and satisfying dish with the classic flavors of Mediterranean cuisine. The marinated and grilled pork, combined with the cool and refreshing Tzatziki sauce, creates a perfect balance of textures and tastes. Assemble the gyro with your favorite toppings for an authentic and flavorful Greek experience. Enjoy this dish for a delightful lunch or dinner that captures the essence of Greek street food!

Teriyaki Pineapple Pork Kebabs

Ingredients:

For the Teriyaki Marinade:

- 1/2 cup soy sauce
- 1/4 cup pineapple juice
- 1/4 cup brown sugar
- 2 tablespoons rice vinegar
- 2 tablespoons mirin (sweet rice wine)
- 2 tablespoons sesame oil
- 2 cloves garlic, minced
- 1 teaspoon fresh ginger, grated
- 1 tablespoon cornstarch (optional, for thickening)

For the Pork Kebabs:

- 1.5 pounds pork loin or pork tenderloin, cut into cubes
- Fresh pineapple, cut into chunks
- Bell peppers, cut into chunks (assorted colors)
- Red onion, cut into chunks

Instructions:

In a bowl, whisk together soy sauce, pineapple juice, brown sugar, rice vinegar, mirin, sesame oil, minced garlic, and grated ginger to make the teriyaki marinade. If you prefer a thicker marinade, you can add cornstarch and mix until well combined.
Place the cubed pork in a resealable plastic bag or shallow dish.
Pour half of the teriyaki marinade over the pork, ensuring all pieces are well-coated. Reserve the other half for basting and serving.
Marinate the pork in the refrigerator for at least 30 minutes to allow the flavors to infuse.
Preheat your grill or grill pan to medium-high heat.
Thread marinated pork cubes, pineapple chunks, bell pepper chunks, and red onion chunks onto skewers, alternating the ingredients.
Grill the kebabs for about 10-15 minutes, turning occasionally, or until the pork is cooked through and has a nice char on the edges.
During grilling, baste the kebabs with the reserved teriyaki marinade for added flavor.
Once cooked, remove the Teriyaki Pineapple Pork Kebabs from the grill and let them rest for a few minutes.

Serve the kebabs with rice or noodles, and drizzle with any remaining teriyaki marinade.

Enjoy the delicious Teriyaki Pineapple Pork Kebabs with the perfect balance of sweet and savory flavors!

These Teriyaki Pineapple Pork Kebabs are a delightful combination of juicy pork, sweet pineapple, and savory teriyaki marinade. Grilling imparts a smoky flavor to the kebabs, making them a perfect dish for outdoor gatherings or barbecue events. Serve them with rice or noodles for a complete meal, and enjoy the delicious harmony of flavors in every bite!

Cuban Picadillo with Ground Pork

Ingredients:

- 1 pound ground pork
- 1 onion, finely chopped

- 3 cloves garlic, minced
- 1 bell pepper, finely chopped
- 1/2 cup green olives, chopped
- 1/2 cup raisins
- 1 can (8 ounces) tomato sauce
- 1 teaspoon ground cumin
- 1 teaspoon dried oregano
- 1/2 teaspoon ground cinnamon
- Salt and black pepper, to taste
- 1/4 cup capers, drained
- 2 tablespoons white wine vinegar
- 2 tablespoons olive oil
- Cooked white rice, for serving
- Fresh cilantro or parsley, chopped (for garnish)

Instructions:

In a large skillet or pan, heat olive oil over medium heat.
Add chopped onions and bell pepper. Sauté until softened, about 3-4 minutes.
Add minced garlic and cook for an additional 1-2 minutes until fragrant.
Add ground pork to the skillet. Break it apart with a spoon and cook until browned.
Stir in ground cumin, dried oregano, ground cinnamon, salt, and black pepper. Mix well to coat the meat with the spices.
Add chopped green olives, raisins, and capers to the skillet. Mix to distribute evenly.
Pour in the tomato sauce and white wine vinegar. Stir the mixture well.
Simmer the Cuban Picadillo for about 15-20 minutes, allowing the flavors to meld and the sauce to thicken.
Taste and adjust the seasoning if needed.
Once cooked, remove the skillet from the heat.
Serve the Cuban Picadillo over cooked white rice.
Garnish with chopped fresh cilantro or parsley.
Enjoy this flavorful Cuban Picadillo with Ground Pork as a comforting and savory dish!

Cuban Picadillo is a classic dish that brings together a delicious combination of savory and sweet flavors. The ground pork, seasoned with spices, olives, raisins, and capers, creates a rich and satisfying meal. Serve it over white rice for a complete and hearty experience. This Cuban Picadillo with Ground Pork is sure to become a family favorite with its comforting and flavorful profile!

Mustard and Herb Crusted Pork Loin

Ingredients:

- 1 3-4 pound boneless pork loin roast
- Salt and black pepper, to taste
- 2 tablespoons Dijon mustard

- 2 tablespoons whole-grain mustard
- 2 tablespoons honey
- 2 tablespoons olive oil
- 2 cloves garlic, minced
- 1 tablespoon fresh rosemary, chopped
- 1 tablespoon fresh thyme, chopped
- 1 tablespoon fresh parsley, chopped
- 1 cup breadcrumbs (panko or regular)
- 2 tablespoons melted butter

Instructions:

Preheat your oven to 375°F (190°C).
Season the pork loin roast with salt and black pepper.
In a small bowl, mix together Dijon mustard, whole-grain mustard, honey, olive oil, minced garlic, chopped rosemary, chopped thyme, and chopped parsley to make the mustard and herb mixture.
Rub the mustard and herb mixture all over the surface of the pork loin, ensuring it is evenly coated.
In a separate bowl, combine breadcrumbs with melted butter to create the breadcrumb mixture.
Press the breadcrumb mixture onto the mustard and herb-coated pork loin, creating a crust.
Place the pork loin in a roasting pan or on a baking sheet.
Roast in the preheated oven for about 1 to 1.5 hours or until the internal temperature reaches 145°F (63°C), basting occasionally with pan juices.
If the crust begins to brown too quickly, you can tent the pork loin with aluminum foil.
Once cooked, remove the Mustard and Herb Crusted Pork Loin from the oven and let it rest for about 10 minutes before slicing.
Slice the pork loin and serve it with any remaining pan juices.
Enjoy the Mustard and Herb Crusted Pork Loin with your favorite side dishes!

This Mustard and Herb Crusted Pork Loin is a delicious and elegant option for a special dinner. The combination of Dijon and whole-grain mustards, honey, and fresh herbs creates a flavorful crust that adds depth to the succulent pork loin. Serve it with your favorite sides for a complete and satisfying meal. Whether for a festive occasion or a family dinner, this dish is sure to impress with its savory and aromatic profile!

Spicy Mango Glazed Pork Chops

Ingredients:

For the Spicy Mango Glaze:

- 1 ripe mango, peeled and diced

- 2 tablespoons soy sauce
- 2 tablespoons honey
- 1 tablespoon rice vinegar
- 1 teaspoon Sriracha sauce (adjust to taste)
- 1 teaspoon fresh ginger, grated
- 2 cloves garlic, minced

For the Pork Chops:

- 4 bone-in pork chops
- Salt and black pepper, to taste
- 2 tablespoons vegetable oil

Instructions:

For the Spicy Mango Glaze:

In a blender or food processor, combine diced mango, soy sauce, honey, rice vinegar, Sriracha sauce, grated ginger, and minced garlic.
Blend until smooth and well combined. If the mixture is too thick, you can add a splash of water to reach your desired consistency.
Taste the glaze and adjust the sweetness or spiciness if needed. Set aside.

For the Pork Chops:

Preheat your grill or grill pan to medium-high heat.
Season the pork chops with salt and black pepper on both sides.
Brush the pork chops with vegetable oil to prevent sticking on the grill.
Grill the pork chops for about 4-5 minutes per side, or until they reach your desired level of doneness.
During the last few minutes of grilling, baste the pork chops generously with the Spicy Mango Glaze, turning them to coat evenly.
Optional: For a caramelized finish, you can place the glazed pork chops under the broiler for a minute or two, keeping a close eye to prevent burning.
Once cooked, remove the Spicy Mango Glazed Pork Chops from the grill and let them rest for a few minutes.
Serve the glazed pork chops with any remaining Spicy Mango Glaze drizzled on top.

Enjoy the Spicy Mango Glazed Pork Chops with a burst of sweet, spicy, and tropical flavors!

These Spicy Mango Glazed Pork Chops offer a delightful combination of sweet and spicy notes, creating a tropical twist to a classic grilled dish. The mango glaze adds a burst of freshness and complexity to the succulent pork chops. Serve them with your favorite sides for a delicious and memorable meal that's perfect for summer grilling or any occasion!

Chipotle BBQ Pulled Pork Nachos

Ingredients:

For the Chipotle BBQ Pulled Pork:

- 2 pounds pork shoulder or pork butt
- Salt and black pepper, to taste
- 1 tablespoon vegetable oil
- 1 onion, diced
- 3 cloves garlic, minced
- 1 can (14 ounces) crushed tomatoes
- 1/2 cup barbecue sauce
- 2 chipotle peppers in adobo sauce, minced
- 1 tablespoon adobo sauce (from the chipotle peppers)
- 1 teaspoon ground cumin
- 1 teaspoon smoked paprika
- 1/2 cup chicken broth

For the Nachos:

- Tortilla chips
- Shredded Monterey Jack and cheddar cheese blend
- Black beans, drained and rinsed
- Diced tomatoes
- Sliced jalapeños
- Sour cream
- Guacamole
- Fresh cilantro, chopped

Instructions:

For the Chipotle BBQ Pulled Pork:

Preheat your oven to 325°F (163°C).
Season the pork shoulder or pork butt with salt and black pepper.
In a large oven-safe Dutch oven or skillet, heat vegetable oil over medium-high heat.
Sear the pork on all sides until browned.
Remove the pork from the pot and set it aside.
In the same pot, add diced onion and sauté until softened.
Add minced garlic and cook for an additional 1-2 minutes until fragrant.
Pour in crushed tomatoes, barbecue sauce, minced chipotle peppers, adobo sauce, ground cumin, smoked paprika, and chicken broth. Stir well to combine.

Return the seared pork to the pot, nestling it into the tomato mixture.
Cover the pot with a lid and transfer it to the preheated oven.
Bake for about 3 to 3.5 hours, or until the pork is tender and easily shreds with a fork.
Once cooked, remove the pork from the pot and shred it using two forks.

For the Nachos:

Preheat your oven broiler.
Arrange tortilla chips on a large baking sheet.
Sprinkle a generous amount of shredded Monterey Jack and cheddar cheese blend over the tortilla chips.
Add the shredded Chipotle BBQ Pulled Pork on top of the cheese.
Scatter black beans, diced tomatoes, and sliced jalapeños over the nachos.
Place the baking sheet under the broiler for 2-3 minutes, or until the cheese is melted and bubbly.
Remove the nachos from the oven and garnish with dollops of sour cream, guacamole, and chopped fresh cilantro.
Serve the Chipotle BBQ Pulled Pork Nachos immediately and enjoy!

These Chipotle BBQ Pulled Pork Nachos are a crowd-pleasing and flavor-packed dish that combines the smoky and spicy goodness of chipotle barbecue pulled pork with the cheesy and crunchy delight of nachos. Perfect for game day or casual gatherings, these nachos are sure to be a hit. Customize with your favorite toppings and enjoy the bold and satisfying flavors!

Herb-Marinated Pork Skewers

Ingredients:

For the Marinade:

- 1/4 cup olive oil

- 2 tablespoons soy sauce
- 2 tablespoons balsamic vinegar
- 2 tablespoons honey
- 3 cloves garlic, minced
- 1 tablespoon fresh rosemary, finely chopped
- 1 tablespoon fresh thyme, finely chopped
- 1 tablespoon fresh parsley, finely chopped
- 1 teaspoon Dijon mustard
- Salt and black pepper, to taste

For the Pork Skewers:

- 1.5 pounds pork tenderloin, cut into 1-inch cubes
- Bell peppers, cut into chunks (assorted colors)
- Red onion, cut into chunks
- Cherry tomatoes
- Wooden or metal skewers

Instructions:

In a bowl, whisk together olive oil, soy sauce, balsamic vinegar, honey, minced garlic, chopped rosemary, chopped thyme, chopped parsley, Dijon mustard, salt, and black pepper to create the marinade.
Place the pork tenderloin cubes in a resealable plastic bag or shallow dish.
Pour the marinade over the pork, ensuring all pieces are well-coated. Seal the bag or cover the dish and refrigerate for at least 2 hours, or overnight for maximum flavor.
If using wooden skewers, soak them in water for about 30 minutes to prevent burning during grilling.
Preheat your grill or grill pan to medium-high heat.
Thread marinated pork cubes, bell pepper chunks, red onion chunks, and cherry tomatoes onto the skewers, alternating the ingredients.
Grill the skewers for about 10-12 minutes, turning occasionally, or until the pork is cooked through and has a nice char on the edges.
Optional: Baste the skewers with any remaining marinade during grilling for added flavor.
Once cooked, remove the Herb-Marinated Pork Skewers from the grill and let them rest for a few minutes.

Serve the skewers with your favorite side dishes.
Enjoy the Herb-Marinated Pork Skewers with the delightful blend of fresh herbs and savory marinade!

These Herb-Marinated Pork Skewers are a perfect choice for a flavorful and aromatic grilling experience. The combination of fresh rosemary, thyme, and parsley, along with the sweet and savory marinade, adds depth to the tender pork. Serve these skewers with a side of your favorite vegetables or rice for a complete and satisfying meal. Enjoy the delicious infusion of herbs in every bite!

Cajun Dirty Rice with Ground Pork

Ingredients:

- 1 pound ground pork
- 1 cup white rice
- 2 cups chicken broth

- 1 onion, finely chopped
- 1 bell pepper, finely chopped
- 2 celery stalks, finely chopped
- 3 cloves garlic, minced
- 1 cup chicken livers, finely chopped
- 1/2 cup green onions, chopped
- 1/4 cup fresh parsley, chopped
- 2 tablespoons vegetable oil
- 1 tablespoon Cajun seasoning (adjust to taste)
- Salt and black pepper, to taste

Instructions:

Rinse the rice under cold water until the water runs clear.

In a medium saucepan, combine the rinsed rice and chicken broth. Bring to a boil, then reduce the heat to low, cover, and simmer until the rice is cooked and the liquid is absorbed.

In a large skillet, heat vegetable oil over medium-high heat.

Add ground pork to the skillet and cook until browned.

Add chopped onion, bell pepper, celery, and minced garlic to the skillet. Sauté until the vegetables are softened.

Add chicken livers to the skillet and cook until they are no longer pink.

Stir in cooked rice, green onions, chopped parsley, and Cajun seasoning. Mix well to combine.

Season with salt and black pepper to taste. Adjust the Cajun seasoning if needed.

Cook the dirty rice mixture for an additional 5-7 minutes, allowing the flavors to meld.

Optional: For added richness, you can stir in a small amount of chicken broth or butter.

Remove the Cajun Dirty Rice with Ground Pork from the heat.

Serve hot, garnished with additional green onions and parsley if desired.

Enjoy this flavorful Cajun Dirty Rice with Ground Pork as a delicious and hearty dish!

Cajun Dirty Rice is a classic Louisiana dish known for its flavorful combination of ground meat, rice, and a variety of seasonings. This version with ground pork adds a rich and savory element to the dish. The Cajun seasoning, along with the "holy trinity" of onions, bell peppers, and celery, gives the rice a spicy and aromatic kick. Serve this Cajun Dirty Rice with Ground Pork as a main dish or as a side to complement your favorite Cajun or Creole meals.

Apple Sage Stuffed Pork Chops

Ingredients:

For the Apple Sage Stuffing:

- 1 cup breadcrumbs
- 1 large apple, peeled, cored, and diced
- 1/2 cup finely chopped onion
- 2 tablespoons butter
- 1/4 cup chopped fresh sage leaves
- 1/4 cup chopped fresh parsley
- Salt and black pepper, to taste

For the Pork Chops:

- 4 thick-cut pork chops
- Salt and black pepper, to taste
- 1 tablespoon olive oil

Instructions:

For the Apple Sage Stuffing:

In a skillet, melt butter over medium heat.
Add chopped onions and sauté until softened.
Add diced apples to the skillet and cook until they begin to soften.
Stir in breadcrumbs, chopped sage, chopped parsley, salt, and black pepper. Cook for an additional 2-3 minutes, allowing the flavors to meld. Remove from heat and let the stuffing cool.

For the Pork Chops:

Preheat your oven to 375°F (190°C).
Using a sharp knife, create a pocket in each pork chop by cutting a slit horizontally along one side.
Season the pork chops with salt and black pepper, both inside the pocket and on the outside.
Stuff each pork chop with the cooled Apple Sage Stuffing, pressing it down gently.
Heat olive oil in an oven-safe skillet over medium-high heat.
Sear the stuffed pork chops on both sides until they develop a golden-brown crust.

Transfer the skillet to the preheated oven and roast for about 20-25 minutes, or until the internal temperature of the pork reaches 145°F (63°C).

Optional: For a caramelized finish, you can broil the stuffed pork chops for a few minutes after roasting, keeping a close eye to prevent burning.

Once cooked, remove the Apple Sage Stuffed Pork Chops from the oven and let them rest for 5-10 minutes before serving.

Serve the stuffed pork chops with any remaining stuffing and your favorite side dishes.

Enjoy these Apple Sage Stuffed Pork Chops for a delightful blend of sweet and savory flavors!

These Apple Sage Stuffed Pork Chops offer a delicious combination of savory pork, sweet apples, and aromatic sage. The stuffing adds a flavorful and comforting element to the juicy pork chops. Serve them with roasted vegetables, mashed potatoes, or a side of your choice for a hearty and satisfying meal. This dish is perfect for a special dinner or any occasion where you want to impress with a delicious and elegant pork dish.

www.ingramcontent.com/pod-product-compliance
Lightning Source LLC
LaVergne TN
LVHW061938070526
838199LV00060B/3865